NORFOLK RECORD SOCIETY

founded 1930

THE NOTEBOOK OF

ROBERT DOUGHTY

1662-1665

edited by
James M. Rosenheim

Norfolk Record Society

Volume LIV

1989

ISBN 0 9511600 4 4

Designed and Printed in Great Britain by
The National Library of Wales, Aberystwyth

CONTENTS

ACKNOWLEDGEMENTS

I am grateful to the Norfolk Record Office and the Norfolk County Council for permission to publish this transcription of the notebook of Robert Doughty.

I originally undertook this edition at the urging of Victor Morgan and A. Hassell Smith, and I have benefited from discussions with them and with Anthony Fletcher about Robert Doughty and his notebook. The staff of the Norfolk Record Office have unfailingly assisted me throughout this project. The College of Liberal Arts at Texas A & M University provided generous support toward publication. Ann Todd Baum and Lester Brown assisted with the proofreading, and my colleague Larry Yarak offered trenchant and constructive comments on the introduction.

INTRODUCTION

The process of criminal justice in the seventeenth century has received extensive scrutiny in recent years, although far more for the first half of the century than for the second. As a result of inquiries made into institutions as varied as the assize courts and the office of village constable, ranging from Cheshire and Westmorland to Surrey and Sussex, a detailed understanding has emerged of how the actions of individuals brought them into contact with the edifice of the law.[1] Regardless of the reality of wrongdoing, the perceived transgression of the law set in motion a 'process of decision-making that turned grievances into accusations, accusations into indictments and indictments into crimes.'[2] A vast array of characters figured in this process (and could bring it to a halt), and scholars have recently elucidated the instrumental role played by the middling and lesser sort of people in constructing and ensuring the community's civic peace. The formal cases that appear to be the irreducible components for re-constructing early modern criminal history, and which led historians to focus on magistrates as the most significant actors in the judicial drama, would not have come into being without the initiative and co-operation of individuals well down the social scale.

Nonetheless, for all this corrective emphasis on the legal system's inclusiveness and its responsiveness to women and men of moderate social status, the fact remains that the justice of the peace, even though his activities were in many ways passive, occupied a pivotal position in the procedures of the law. It was after all before a justice of the peace that a grievance crossed the line from a private to a public matter. Others 'could activate the machinery of legal administration, but they could neither move beyond it nor drop accusations once made, without the help of a magistrate.'[3] Of course, many matters presented to the justice ended in mediation and went no further, and in this sense they remained unofficial. Moreover, drawing a line between private, personalized mediation and public, administrative process, between official and unofficial response, is to attempt a formal distinction among different activities that is difficult to make whether examining the past or the modern world. Even so, it was before the justice that misunderstandings and quarrels and even violence between individuals took on material substance by being set down in a permanent form. The significance of recording grievances on paper, an action which the justice and his clerk took, should especially not be ignored in a society where literacy remained a restricted skill. It is not surprising that so many historians have focussed on the magistrate as the key player in the criminal drama, for the paper trail began with him.

Robert Doughty of Hanworth (1616/1617 - 1670) held office as a justice of the peace under Charles II for less than five years, from late 1660 until October 1665.[4] A member of a lesser gentry family from north-east Norfolk, he was placed on the commission of the peace in December 1660. His name appears on parliamentary tax commissions for Norfolk beginning in 1652, and he may have performed judicial service late in the commonwealth period.[5] His delayed appointment to the magistracy six months after the restoration perhaps indicates that the central government initially hesitated because of his political past and then named him to the bench because of his prior experience. Once appointed, Doughty served avidly, perhaps even with an excess of zeal. His dismissal in October 1665 (of which he apparently remained unaware for weeks, since he continued to act as a justice into December) resulted partly from his activities off the bench as a tax commissioner who offended an influential Norfolk squire. Yet his work as a justice also 'sufficiently affronted' his colleagues on the bench so as to justify his displacement.[6]

The notebook Doughty kept from 1662 to 1665 exemplifies his energetic application to the duties of magistracy. It also illustrates the formal and informal ways in which a local magistrate determined the outcome of particular legal processes. In a record that grows progressively detailed over time, Doughty can repeatedly be seen to choose among various options open to him in managing the complaints he confronted. Some parties were merely bound to keep the peace toward one another and quickly dismissed; others were bound by recognizances meant to ensure their appearance at sessions and their good behaviour in the meantime; still others were ordered to gaol. From his seat at Hanworth, where the vast bulk of his business was conducted, Doughty sorted among accusations, sifted good evidence from bad, reconciled conflicting stories, and ultimately served a critical role in determining whether formal prosecution of any particular accusation would take place. After reaching a determination, which often resulted in the issuance of a warrant written out by his clerk Robert Foster and signed and sealed by the justice himself, Doughty then turned to his notebook and recorded his actions there.

Robert Doughty's notebook, currently catalogued as Aylsham 829 in the Norfolk Record Office in Norwich, is a small book measuring just 14.5 cm. by 9.5 cm. It is bound in vellum and contains 94 leaves altogether, although it is only one third full. It is unclear how often Doughty made entries in the book or how soon after the events that they preserved, but variations in handwriting and ink suggest it was a nearly-contemporaneous record. Occasional confusion of dates shows that Doughty was fallible in maintaining his book, and he probably used the generally brief notations more as broad reminders of the decisions he had made than as detailed reconstructions of the matters brought to him. On the other hand, some entries were prolix, and Doughty seems unlikely to have written his extensive accounts of vexing affairs or of cases heard at quarter sessions simply to remind himself of the particulars. Perhaps because the sessions' decisions became precedents binding Doughty and other magistrates, it made good sense to register them, but beyond this we may plausibly credit him with a desire to preserve a record of public events in which he had taken part. The sheer mass of his surviving papers, the existence of the notebook itself, and the character of the entries made there all speak of Doughty's nearly-obsessive seriousness (and his pride) in the performance of his duties as a justice of the peace.

A magistrate's archive like that of Robert Doughty is rare but not unknown.[7] In his case, however, the concurrent survival of his notebook and of literally hundreds of additional official papers affords an exceptional view of the justice's daily business. Even more than does the notebook itself, which in some measure was a necessarily cryptic reference guide, Doughty's surviving warrants, recognizances, depositions and even letters illuminate in overwhelming detail the complaints brought to him — and the society that generated them. The notebook records some 650 occasions upon which Doughty acted as a justice, an average of better than once every two days or 180 each year. This activity far exceeds the pace of William Holcroft in Essex and the burden of even the busiest justice found in late-Stuart Kent (who averaged 150 cases per year), because unlike the latter magistrate's business, which was overwhelmingly *pro forma*, the majority of Doughty's cases required studied and imaginative action.[8]

The notebook, which begins more than a year and a half after Doughty first acted in his capacity as a magistrate,[9] consists largely of a chronicle of his activities as a single justice acting out of sessions. As comprehensive as this chronicle appears, and by contrast with the extensive record of public activities that William Holcroft preserved in his book, Doughty's barely hints at the full story of his public life. Although he carefully preserved the charge he addressed to local tax commissioners in February 1664 (printed below as Appendix II), his notebook does not record the delivery. Indeed, his non-judicial service as tax commissioner receives no coverage there, and despite numerous references among his papers to petty sessions meetings, the notebook preserves his attendance at just two.[10] He does refer to or imply attendance at seven quarter sessions meetings and describes business transacted at several, but official sessions records note his presence at eleven additional meetings, showing that the notebook gives only a partial account of his service on the bench in open court.[11] Nonetheless, business undertaken as a single justice rather than as a participant at quarter sessions comprised the bulk of Doughty's work as a magistrate, yet even here the notebook will not have recorded those occasions when Doughty helped resolve disputes without taking formal action or generating paperwork.[12] How many such interventions occurred cannot be ascertained, although they may have been relatively infrequent if it is true that aggrieved parties generally approached a magistrate when they believed they had a case to make and thus sought official sanction for an investigation they already had in hand.[13] The informal business of mediation therefore may have merited no permanent record in the notebook. Doughty certainly omitted recording much routine administration, such as passing the accounts of overseers of the poor or swearing new parish officers.[14] And cases that originated with another justice but later came to Doughty's notice seem to have been set down more or less indifferently: some are recorded, some not.[15] Beyond these examples, Doughty's papers include evidence of occasions when he took official action as a justice in criminal matters but simply made no entry in his notebook.[16]

While his notebook provides an incomplete account even of his judicial activities, Robert Doughty nonetheless noted therein the four occasions during his tenure on the bench when he delivered the charge to the quarter sessions grand jury. Three of these addresses survive, along with notes that may have been meant for the fourth, and the complete charges are printed in Appendix I.[17] Delivering the charge was an honour usually reserved for a distinguished justice, although in Norfolk, where sessions were held every quarter in each of the county's three divisions, the distinction was somewhat diminished outside the Norwich meeting, the most prestigious and best-attended gathering of the three. Nonetheless, it is puzzling that Doughty received the responsibility of delivering the charge yet never became a member of the quorum on the commission of the peace: presumably the same qualifications of learning in the law that warranted one distinction would have merited the other.

As has been observed by one student of Doughty's papers, his charges were 'suffused with the propaganda of order.'[18] Unlike the speeches delivered by a contemporary in Cheshire, Sir Peter Leicester, Doughty's were rather legalistic disquisitions.[19] He evidently relied on William Lambarde's *Eirenarcha*[20] for themes, organization and even phraseology, and he displayed no conspicuous concern with political theory or philosophy. Rather, he focussed on the jurors in his audience, emphasizing their obligations and enumerating the more common crimes they might encounter. More significantly, he offered historical explanations for current procedures, justifying while also extolling the virtues of the common law. He also dwelt on matters of current import, whether those raised at recent quarter sessions or by his personal experience. Pedestrian in content, Doughty's charges are significant for the insight they provide into the immediate concerns of the justice. Where Sir Peter Leicester's 'curious series' of lectures was intended as a set of homilies directed at the justices rather than the jurymen,[21] Doughty kept the more humble in his audience squarely in view, claiming (perhaps disingenuously) that he was best qualified to address the 'raw bystanders' in the court. Almost invariably practical in his presentation, if sometimes long-winded, he chided jurors for their dilatory appearance, explained the nature of new statutory offences and stressed the significance of the jury's part in the effective enforcement of the law. While his long explanations about ways to discern fraudulent passes or to identify former thieves may have helped fellow-magistrates in their interrogations, they simultaneously aided parish officers in making discoveries and juries in assessing the plausibility of indictments.

As does his notebook, Doughty's charges lay bare the multi-faceted elements of magisterial office. Moralizing combined with generous understanding of human failures, flexibility with rigidity, paternalism with co-operation. His ability to govern in his community was limited by a wide number of factors, including his dependence on deference and good will (neither of which were always forthcoming) from the county and parish officers as well as from common citizens, all of whom played essential parts in implementing his decisions. The deleterious limitations he believed were placed on his own authority as a justice of the peace also restrained Doughty, as did the vagaries of political power. The last seem finally to have brought his dismissal, as he grew unpopular with his fellow magistrates and ultimately with Norfolk's lord lieutenant for his pedantic and particular ways. Thus the picture presented here of Robert Doughty is not of rural autocrat dispensing roughshod justice on the unfortunates of the surrounding community. Rather, he is a conscientious player, but only one of many, in the complicated network of decision-making and persuasion, of command and compromise, that made up the fabric of the administration of seventeenth-century law.

Notes to the Introduction

1. See among other works J. S. Cockburn, *A History of English Assizes 1558-1714*, Cambridge, 1972; J. S. Morrill, *The Cheshire Grand Jury 1625-1659: A Social and Administrative Study*, Leicester University, Department of English Local History, Occasional Papers, 3rd series, no. 1, Leicester, 1976; A. Macfarlane, *The Justice and the Mare's Ale: Law and disorder in seventeenth-century England*, Oxford, 1981; N. Landau, *The Justices of the Peace, 1679-1760*, Berkeley, 1984; J. Kent, *The English Village Constable 1580-1642: A Social and Administrative Study*, Oxford, 1986; J. M. Beattie, *Crime and the Courts in England 1660-1800*, Oxford, 1986; C. B. Herrup, *The Common Peace: Participation and the criminal law in seventeenth-century England*, Cambridge, 1987.
2. Herrup, p. 9.
3. Herrup, p. 86.
4. The following account of RD is based on J. M. Rosenheim, 'Robert Doughty of Hanworth: A Restoration Magistrate,' *Norfolk Archaeology*, 38, pt. 3 (1983), pp. 296-312. RD also figures frequently in A. Fletcher, *Reform in the Provinces: The Government of Stuart England*, New Haven, 1986.
5. A Robert Doughty was added to the Norfolk commission of the peace in July 1657: Public Record Office, C 231/6, ff. 372, 377. No evidence confirms that this was RD of Hanworth rather than his cousin of Aylsham. A tax commission of 1650 includes Robert Doughty of Aylsham; ones for 1652, 1657 and January 1660 simply list Robert Doughty: C. H. Firth and R. S. Rait, *Acts and Ordinances of the Interregnum 1642-1660* (3 vols., London, 1911), ii, 472, 670-1, 1075-6, 1375.
6. The phrase is that of the lord lieutenant, Lord Townshend, in an undated, unaddressed draft to 'My Lord' (perhaps to the Lord Chancellor), which requested RD's dismissal from the bench: Raynham Hall, Norfolk, uncatalogued manuscripts, correspondence of Horatio, first viscount Townshend. I am grateful to the Marquess Townshend for permission to consult the manuscripts at Raynham.
7. J. A. Sharpe, for example, has recently edited the papers of William Holcroft of Essex, whose career in public office ranged from 1662 to 1689: *'William Holcroft, His Booke': Local office-holding in late Stuart Essex*, Essex Historical Documents: 2 (Essex Record Office Publication No. 90), Chelmsford, 1986.

8. For Kent, see Landau, pp. 177-78. To Landau, dealing with three cases per month constituted 'continuous activity' on the part of JPs; RD averaged sixteen cases per month.
9. RD's first surviving official papers are certificates of men taking the oath of allegiance: certificates, 28 January 1661, Norfolk Record Office (hereafter designated 'NRO'; this designation is omitted from subsequent references to the Aylsham collection), Aylsham 1.
10. RD's papers concerning the assessment and collection of taxes in the 1660s are found in Aylsham 193, 306 and 307. RD also served as a commissioner in a chancery suit: British Library, Add. MS 27967, f. 84. For petty sessions see entries for 21 April 1663 and 28 March 1665.
11. NRO, C/S2/2 and C/S1/8; the total of eighteen meetings is one more than the figure given in Rosenheim, p. 299.
12. Almost all the notebook entries record the issuance of a warrant for some specific purpose.
13. For this suggestion, see Herrup, chap. 4, which examines the progression from 'crime to criminal accusation'.
14. See certificates concerning Antingham overseers' accounts, 8 May 1663; churchwardens and constables at Norwood Barningham, 9 May 1663; a constable of Beeston Regis, 21 October 1663; and a constable of Gimingham, 12 July 1664, all in Aylsham 347 and all unrecorded in the notebook.
15. Omissions seem to have been unaffected by whether the case was begun by the other justice alone or jointly with RD. See Sir John Palgrave's warrant, 5 May 1663, Aylsham 1 (endorsed with RD's notes concerning the appearance before him of the person named in the warrant) and also a joint warrant by RD and Palgrave, 21 May 1663, Aylsham 347. Neither is recorded in the notebook.
16. For example, see warrants for the appearance of John Fisher, 8 July 1663; of Henry Harrison, 30 September 1663; of Thomas Strike, 12 May 1665; of John Dun, 21 September 1665; of Gregory and Thomas Harper, 4 November 1665; and information of Nicholas Allen, 24 June 1665, all in Aylsham 347. The absence of entries concerning conventicles that RD ordered suppressed is especially intriguing: see warrants of 7 May 1665, British Library, Additional MS 27967, fols. 83-83v and Aylsham 1; papers of 11 and 16 June 1665, ibid.; and of 11 June 1665, Aylsham 193. See also Public Record Office, ASSI 16/11/5, with a record of five men RD bound to appear at Norwich assizes in July 1665, charged with non-attendance at church and failure to take requisite oaths.
17. For the fourth charge see notes beginning 'In the year of our Lord 1348,' Aylsham 304.
18. Fletcher, p. 172 and pp. 116-75 on charges generally.
19. Sir Peter Leicester, *Charges to the Grand Jury at Quarter Sessions 1660-1677*, E. M. Halcrow, ed., *Chetham Society*, 3rd ser., 5 (1953). Cf. also Beattie's account of the charges of Sir More Molyneux in the 1730s: *Crime and the Courts*, p. 332.
20. W. Lambarde, *Eirenarcha, or Of the Office of the Justice of Peace*, London, 1619.
21. Morrill, p. 23.

A NOTE ON STYLE AND TRANSCRIPTION

The following conventions have been adopted throughout this transcription. Dates are in Old Style, except that the year is taken to begin on 1 January. Spelling and punctuation have been modernized and place names rendered in their modern form. Christian name spellings have been modernized and their unambiguous abbreviations expanded. Surnames are as in the original, even where spelling varies within a given entry of the notebook. Where surnames are spelled differently in supporting documents, the notebook's spelling has been retained in the notes, but significant variations are indicated. The names of Robert Doughty's fellow justices, usually indicated only by initials in the notebook, have been expanded in the text. These justices have been identified in the notes the first time they are mentioned. Single letters used in the text to denote towns of residence that are identifiable from supporting documents have also been silently expanded, as have common contemporary abbreviations. The abbreviation 'li.' has been rendered by '£' and '&c.' by 'etc.'

Round brackets appear in the original. The notebook's few textual insertions and marginalia have been incorporated in the text. Deletions in the original have been indicated in the notes. Editorial additions are indicated throughout in square brackets, and residences and personal qualifications found in supporting documents are added to the text in this way. Uncertain expansions and questionable readings of partly legible words have been shown by the use of square brackets with a question mark. Blanks in the original have been indicated as '[blank]'. Dates, whether in English or Latin, have been expanded, except in the instance of those dates given as a combination of numeral and letters, i.e. '7bris'. Figures throughout have been rendered in Arabic. Unless otherwise specified, the date of surviving documents cited in the notes is the same as that of the notebook entry to which they relate. In the notes, Robert Doughty has been referred to as 'RD'.

THE NOTEBOOK OF ROBERT DOUGHTY

[f. 1r] The oath of a witness.

You shall true answer make to all such questions as I shall demand of you concerning this matter or offence now before me, wherein you shall say the whole truth and nothing but the truth, and so help you God.

The oath of one who sweareth the peace.

You shall swear that you require not the peace against A B for any private malice, hatred or evil will, but for that you are afraid (he or she) will burn your houses, kill, maim or otherwise do you some bodily harm, and so help you God.

The oath of a petty constable.

You shall swear that you shall well & truly serve our sovereign lord the king in the office of a constable in the town of [blank] as the same was originally constituted and hath not since been altered. You shall see his majesty's peace to be well and duly kept and preserved there. You shall duly present all and every the offences you shall know done in the said town while you continue in the said office contrary to the statutes made in the first (chapter the ninth), fourth (chapter the first), and the one and twentieth (chapter the seventh) years of the reign of King James of late memory, or [contrary] to any of them, for restraining the inordinate haunting and tippling in inns, alehouses & victualling houses, and for repressing of drunkenness, or for either of them. And you shall well and duly according to your knowledge, power and ability do and execute all other things you are bound to observe or do under your oath as a constable so long as you continue a constable there, and so help you God.

[f. 1v] The oath of a chief constable.

You shall swear that you shall well and truly serve our sovereign lord the king's majesty in the office of one of the chief constables of the hundred of [blank]. You shall endeavour to the uttermost of your power to see the king's majesty's peace to be kept in the said hundred and shall well and duly according to your knowledge, power & ability do and execute all other things you are bound to observe or do under your oath as a chief constable so long as you continue in the said office, and so help you God.

The oaths to convict an unlicensed alehousekeeper.

Either of you for yourself shall swear that A B of C in the county of Norfolk, gentleman, have in C aforesaid upon his (or her) own authority not being thereunto lawfully licensed lately taken upon him (or her) to keep a common alehouse (or) tippling house (or) use commonly selling beer, ale, cider or perry, & that this is the first offence of this nature he hath been convicted of. And so God respectively help either of you. [One word illegible] & 6 Edward VI, c. 25. (Two justices). 1 by 3 Charles [I], c. 3. 20s. [fine].

The oath to convict a person of drunkenness.

You[1] shall swear that A B of C in the county of Norfolk, blacksmith, on Monday now last past in C aforesaid was drunk, and so God help you.[2] ([Word illegible] & 1 J.) 4 James c. 5 & 21 [James] c. 7. [To be prosecuted] within 6 months; 5s. [fine].

The oaths of the witnesses to convict any person of profane cursing (or) swearing.

Either of you for yourself shall swear that A B of C in the county of Norfolk, yeoman, did on Thursday last past in C aforesaid profanely curse (or) swear in these words, The devil take you (or) by God's wounds, and so God respectively help either one of you. 21 James c. 20. [To be prosecuted] within 20 days; 12d. [fine].

The oath of the witness to convict tipplers in taverns, inns, alehouses or victualling houses.

[f. 2r] You shall swear that A B of C in the county of Norfolk, labourer, D E of F in the county aforesaid, gunsmith, & H I of F aforesaid, sailor, did on Friday now last past in C aforesaid by the space of two hours together remain or continue tippling or drinking in the inn, alehouse, or victualling house of K L of C aforesaid, taverner, contrary to the statutes in such case made & provided, and so help you God. [To be prosecuted] within six months; 3s. 4d. [fine].

The oath of a witness to convict a taverner, innkeeper, victualer or alehousekeeper.

You shall swear that A B of C in the county of Norfolk, taverner, did on Friday now last past in C aforesaid utter & sell less than one full ale quart of the best beer for a penny (or) of the small beer for an half penny, [the fine being] 20s. (or) permit & suffer R S, T V and W X, being all three of D in the county aforesaid, sailors, to remain & continue tippling or drinking in his house contrary to the statutes in such case made & provided [the fine being] 10s., and so help you God. 1 James c. 9, 4 James c. 4 & 5, 21 James c. 7, 1 Charles [I] c. 3, 3 Charles [I] c. 3, 7 James c. 10, & 5 Edward VI c. 25.

The oath of a witness against one for not going to church etc. within a month after the default.

You shall swear that A B now & on Sunday now last past of C in the county of Norfolk,[3] tailor, did not on Sunday aforesaid resort or repair to any church, chapel or any other usual place appointed for common prayer & there hear divine service according to the statutes on that behalf made. 12d. [fine].

[fols. 2v-5r are blank]

[f. 5v] *Memorandum:* In Michaelmas term 1660 & [the] twelfth year of his majesty's reign, I Robert Doughty was put into the commission of the peace and was sworn at the Twelfth[-night] sessions then next following. *Memorandum:* Easter sessions & midsummer sessions are for these parts to be held at Fakenham, unless one [of] them be held at Holt. But Michaelmas sessions and Twelfth[-night] sessions are constantly to be held at Little Walsingham.

A note of those [who] have given the charge at each of these sessions ever since I was so sworn:[4]

Twelfth[-night]	1661	12 Charles II	Mr Nicholas Stileman
Easter	1661	13 Charles predicto	Mr Samuel Smith
Midsummer	1661	13 Charles predicto	Mr Simon Brittif
Michaelmas	1661	13 Charles predicto	Mr Samuel Smith
Twelfth[-night]	1662	13 Charles predicto	Mr Edward Pepis
Easter	1662	14 Charles predicto	Mr Samuel Smith
Midsummer	1662	14 Charles predicto	I Robert Doughty
Michaelmas	1662	14 Charles predicto	Mr Nicholas Stileman
Twelfth[-night]	1663	14 Charles predicto	Mr Simon[5] Brittif
Easter	1663	15 Charles predicto	Mr Samuel Smith
Midsummer	1663	15 Charles predicto	Mr Stileman for Mr Pepis
Michaelmas	1663	15 Charles predicto	Mr Robert Doughty
Twelfth[-night]	1664	15 Charles predicto	Mr Nicholas Stileman
Easter	1664	16 Charles predicto	Mr Simon Brittif
Midsummer	1664	16 Charles predicto	Mr Robert Doughty
Michaelmas	1664	16 Charles predicto	Mr Nathaniel Shouldham
Twelfth[-night]	1665	16 Charles predicto	Mr Nicholas Stileman
Easter	1665	17 Charles predicto	Mr Simon Brittif
Midsummer	1665	17 Charles predicto	Mr Robert Doughty

[f. 6r] On Thursday the seventh of August Anno Domini 1662 at the general quarter sessions at Fakenham I gave the charge.[6] The chief matters happening there were three indictments for petty larcenies, whereof the first was of George Parke, a labourer, for stealing two blocks of his master's, which were thought not to be taken feloniously, it being usual (as he said) for woodsellers thereabout to carry home a faggot of rotten wood, & he taking the two blocks which were the great ends of wood then felled in lieu of such a faggot. The second [indictment] was of Margaret Ellys, Ann Gunthorp & Rachel Gunthorp for stealing five pewter plates valued at 10d. of John Cooke, Esq., whose crest was stamped upon them. The two last helped the first to sell them at Hempton Whitsun Fair. The first said she had them for that end of her mother, who acknowledged the same & further said that the same with meat on them were given her at Mr Cooke's. The third [indictment] was of Ann Taylor, another maid, & Barbara Chapman for stealing a salt fish, 6 eggs & two loaves of bread. The master could not swear the goods to be his. The maid said the loaves were Barbara Chapman's & privately baked in her mistress's oven & after she carried them to her, and that she carried her the said salt fish and eggs from her partner for her hose heeling. So if Barbara Chapman were guilty (for she wept during all the trial very bitterly) it was but as accessory, whereas she was indicted as principal. But the jury acquitted all six.

And a traverse of an indictment for stopping up an highway which after a long hearing and some cross swearing was found (the king's witnesses being of best credit). But because we thought it not fit to adjudge the offender forthwith to lay open the way, we respited the setting of the fine until the next sessions, but we then told him that if he did not forthwith lay the same open his fine would be the greater, whereupon he promised forthwith to lay it open.

[f. 6v] I[mprimis?] *9° August 1662:* Upon Mr Augustine Reeve's certificate that Thomas Leasy was chosen at the leet of Aylsham extra Lancaster for the town of Aylsham, I sware him one of the constables there.[7]

11 August: Richard Flaxman [the elder] of Antingham [husbandman] was to be brought before (me only) for extreme beating & bruising Ann Gilbert his maid. He had been before me once before for beating her and had promised to beat her no more. Upon hearing him I ordered him to pay her 5s. for her wages & to deliver her her clothes, & I discharged her his service, 11 August predicto.[8]

Eodem: a warrant against Edmund Tooly of Suffield for refusing to serve Mr [John] Symonds [of same] in his harvest work, being let & having taken 1s. in earnest.[9]

12 August: a warrant for to search in Alby hill for white wheat in the straw stolen off the swath from Robert Fisher, clerk.

Eodem: a warrant to pay Susan Wells, widow, 18d. by the week & 7s. 6d. now in arrear to her from the churchwardens & overseers of Metton.

13 [August]: a warrant for Ambrose[10] Mills, a common alehousekeeper in Hunworth, for committing divers offences against his articles; to appear etc. 15 August.[11]

14 [August]: a warrant for John Bell for to show cause why he departed before the end of his term for which he was retained with John Ward of Felmingham, gentleman.[12]

15 [August]: upon the oaths of Edward Dawson [husbandman] & Elizabeth [wife of John] Kendall both of Hunworth, Ambrose Milles alehousekeeper there was convicted for not selling an ale quart of the best beer for a penny (one churchwarden there).[13]
23 August: a warrant against Katherine Cooke of Gresham for departing the service of Nicholas Smith of Metton before the end of her term.
27 [August]: a warrant against John Hawes of North Walsham, a tapster to Richard Smith an alehousekeeper of North Walsham, upon the oath of Alice Smith his wife for the peace towards them.[14]
28 [August]: a warrant against Amy Spurrell, servant to the said John Hawes, to cause her to come[15] before me with sureties for her good abearing that I may proceed etc.[16]
29º[August]: a warrant to quicken the execution of the two former & to require witnesses to appear to testify their knowledges against the said Amy Spurrell.[17]
30 [August]: a warrant to search for to search [sic] in Metton for barley in the straw stolen off the swath, being the goods of James Taylor, clerk.
9 September: a warrant against Thomas Harnett for beating John Amys [of] Thurgarton.[18]
[f. 7r] *10 [September] 1662:* a warrant to the officers of Suffield to provide for [blank] a poor & lame person.
23 7bris: a warrant at large to apprehend Thomas Gambling of Thwaite, husbandman, for suspicion of breaking the house of Susan Allison and stealing a purse with £7 in the same of Hannah Allison her daughter's & other goods on Sunday next before in the afternoon.[19]
24 [September]: a warrant against the aforesaid Richard Flaxman for not paying the said Ann Gilbert her 5s. & not delivering her her new smock, cost 4s. 2d.[20]
29 [September]: a warrant for William Drury [yeoman] to be sworn constable of Thurgarton.[21]
1 8bris: a warrant against Laurence Archer, being brewer, for making holes in the guilfatt[22] of Jeffrey Flaxman of Aylsham his master.
7 [October]: a warrant against Jeffrey Massy [of Southrepps, husbandman] for getting a bastard on the body of Margaret Tyler of Southrepps [spinster] (her husband [Michael Tyler] went away 5 years since with Captain Reymes), & Massy acknowledged himself to have 3 children but denied to her to have any wife living.[23]
14 [October]: a warrant of the peace against Stephen Durrant who yesterday assaulted Richard Hardingham (both of Suffield) with a pistol & after with a tuck.
Eodem: a warrant against Christian Tuck for suffering card playing in her alehouse & refusing to sell a quart of the best beer for a penny: [in] Antingham.[24]
17 [October]: a warrant for [blank] Bell to be relieved by the overseers of Thurgarton.
21 [October]: a warrant for to provide a house for James Purdy of Saxthorpe poor [person]: 2s.[25]
28 [October]: a warrant for providing a house for the said Purdy and he to pay the rent (and the town [3s.?]).

Eodem: a warrant against Samuel Smith late of Roughton [husbandman] for begetting a bastard on the body of Ellen Woolsey of the same (they are married) (query).[26]
Eodem: a warrant against Joan Bunting for departing the service of Thomas Bacon, her terms not being expired: [in] Gresham.
29 [October]: Richard Allison & Francis Wild sworn constables of Ingworth.[27]
31 [October]: a warrant against Thomas Corke for departing the service of Robert Harmer of Gunton.
1 9bris: a warrant of the peace against Thomas Turner of Southrepps upon the oath of Richard Allen of the same.
2 [November]: a warrant against Edmund Ashwell of Bradfield, carpenter, for not helping to maintain Mary his wife & two children (he lives from his wife).
4 [November]: Frances Barnes sworn constable of Sustead & Richard Allen.
6 [November]: a warrant for Mr William Blofield and Thomas Swift of Runton to be sworn constable, being chosen by the leet there.[28]
[f. 7v] *12 [November] 1662:* Thomas Swift was sworn in the place of Nicholas Dawson.
17 [November]: a warrant against Thomas Simpson of Antingham, labourer, for getting a bastard on the body of Mary Joyce of the same.
Eodem: he was examined & denied the offence & was bound in a recognizance in £10 & Edmund Simpson, worsted weaver, his father, and John Cromer, husbandman, all of Antingham aforesaid, in £5 apiece, conditioned for the said Thomas his appearance at the next sessions etc. & for his good behaviour in the meantime (at the sessions rebound).[29]
Eodem: the said William Blofield for not appearing to be sworn was to be attached.[30]
19 [November]: a warrant of misdemeanour against William Cooper, linen weaver, & Samuel Hinds, labourer, both of Swanton Abbot, & Giles Sprunt, labourer, and John Hamond, labourer, both of Skeyton, for taking 3 cows in the night & in the morning [of] 18 November predicto divers other goods of John Cocke's of Leasingham of the value together of £10 or £12, by pretence of a suit of the said Cooper (as was thought), who after in the presence of Thomas Buttivant of Leasingham did disclaim that he had anything against the said Cock. And it is by them objected against the former four [that] they did the same to gain a promise from the said Cock for the satisfaction of the said Cooper for a debt or debts owing by a brother-in-law of the said Cocke's to the said Cooper. For which Cooper had had a competent security if not satisfaction (would have had him engage for £5 thereof when he would not get such an engagement for the whole as aforesaid) as the said Buttivant affirmed. And wherefore the same were taken or where [and] in whose custody they remain the said Cock & Buttivant cannot discover.
21 [November]: a warrant against John Smith of Blickling for misdemeanour committed (when in drink) at the house of Thomas Porter in Aylsham (threatening to knock his children on the head & breaking his windows) etc.

25 [November]: a warrant to the officers of Banningham to provide an habitation & other relief for Mary Rishford, shut out of her house & ready to starve.
Eodem: a warrant of the peace against George Durrant of Aylsham, labourer, for beating Henry Hewett so as he was lame for a month & threatening him the next day.
29 [November]: a warrant to search in Aldborough fairstead for stall gear stolen from Edmund Duffield of North Walsham, hab[erdasher?] of small wares.
2 [December]: Edmund Cooke, chose at the leet, sworn constable of Thurgarton.
3 [December]: a warrant for Nicholas Pescod & Thomas More to be sworn constables of Colby.[31]
[f. 8r] *3 December 1662:* John Black the only churchwarden & overseer of the poor of the parish of Colby (William Tompson who was the other being lately deceased) did complain unto me that Samuel Bunne, labourer, did on Saturday last come from Alby to settle in a tenement in Colby aforesaid under the yearly value of £10 (where he is an inmate) and that he is likely to be chargeable to the said parish (& had my hand & seal to a warrant which Sir John Palgrave also set his hand & seal unto) but upon his advice I suppressed it.[32]
5 [December]: the said Pescod & More appearing according to my warrant of 3 [December] were sworn.
8 [December]: a warrant to Jer. Blofield, gentleman, to search in Alby for a leather piece & other goods lately stolen from him.
16 [December]: a warrant against Edward Clerke of Southrepps, tailor, for speaking treasonable words against his majesty & against his peace. John Moyses [of Southrepps, tailor] prosecutor.
17 [December]: he was by me & Sir John Palgrave committed to the gaol.[33]
19 [December]: John Cubitt & Thomas Rowland churchwardens & William Purdy & Thomas Rowland overseers of the poor of Southrepps did then make complaint unto me that [blank] Littlewood, widow, a poor woman & likely to be chargeable to the parish of Southrepps did within 40 days last past, vidzt. on the 10th or 11th day of November last past, come to settle in a tenement in Southrepps under the yearly value of £10 (being an outhouse of a tenement wherein her daughter liveth of £4 10s. rent or thereabout) and that she was last legally settled for above the space of 40 days in Thorpe Market as a sojourner and that her said daughter though able doth not give her any further relief than her dwelling in the same tenement & liberty to come to her fire.
24 [December]: a warrant to search for a folgate stolen by William Steele of Roughton.[34]
26 [December]: Sir John Palgrave & myself ordered 12d. a week to Emme Byshop of Holt.
Eodem: we ordered Richard Browne of Gresham firing or money to buy it.
1 January [1663]: a warrant for William Bower [tailor] & his wife to be before me & the coroner at or about Alby church this afternoon to discover how far they or either of them be guilty in the late death of Rebecca Russels their servant.[35]

[f. 8v] *2°January 1663:* a warrant to the churchwardens & overseers of Antingham for the relief of Thomas Blackston & his wife [Ellen, poor persons], being in straits occasioned by their putting Joseph Kirby [worsted weaver] upon them (at a low rate) & by his foul sore on his leg.[36]
6 [January]: Robert Meredith was bound an apprentice by the only surviving churchwarden & overseer of Colby to Henry Bacon of Thurgarton in the trade of a carpenter until his age of 24 years (I & Sir John Palgrave [made the order]).
26 [January]: a warrant against Joseph Witherly of Blickling to answer misdemeanours to be objected by Thomas Pescod a cobbler of Aylsham (for stealing or taking his own boots out of Pescod's shop when Pescod had new soled them, for which he had made Pescod pay 9s. & if found he was to have the 9s. again, 6d. of beer & 16d. for the soles). Witherly's maid Margery Hickes hath discovered he hath them & that they were [muddy?].
Eodem: James Pye of Gresham bound apprentice with R. Foster of Metton.
27 [January]: Thomas Grime & Richard Hodson, churchwardens and overseers of Knapton, complained to me that John Ward [tailor] & his wife (or one he calleth his wife) did within 40 days come from North Walsham where they had been last settled for 40 days. And William Becke, glover, & his wife & Joan Chamberleyne her sister (who is near if not blind) did within the said time come from Binham etc. to settle in several tenements in Knapton whereof neither were of the yearly value of £10. Whereupon they had my several warrants for the respective persons to give sufficient security to discharge Knapton or else to show us cause why they should not be removed back to their former settled places.[37]
31 [January]: a warrant to apprehend Thomas Allen of Aylsham for suspicion of stealing three sheep (one being an ewe & two wethers) of the goods of Thomas Kitchin of Tuttington.
2 February: a warrant against Thomas Copeman for stealing timber of Mr Bell of Alb.[38]
4 [February]: a warrant of the peace against John Roberts of Aylmerton, warrener, for breaking the head of Nicholas Abbes, singleman, of the same.
17 [February]: a warrant (with Sir John Palgrave) to provide house & other relief for Susan Carr & her children to Suffield officers.[39]
20 [February]: a warrant against Robert Duffield of Sustead [kidder] to answer misdemeanours to be objected by Abs & others for stealing vetches (cuiusdem alii ignoti) for I know not whether they were the said Abbes of [blank] or Thaxter's.
22 [February]: William Abbes of Gresham [was bound] in £20 to indict & give evidence against Robert Duffield [kidder] of Sustead for stealing of vetches & John Flaxman [was bound] in £20 that he & Margaret his wife shall give such evidence as either of them knoweth concerning the same stealing of vetches.
[f. 9r] *23 [February]:* Robert Duffield & Henry Gunton [yeoman] of W. & Francis Barnes [blacksmith] of Sustead in £20 and £10 apiece bailed before Sir John Palgrave and myself RD.[40]
At Twelfth[-night] sessions one was indicted for stealing 50s. of another. Upon the evidence it appeared that the 50s. was given by the mother of

the other (to be parted betwixt her & her sister), their father never knowing of it till after the stealing. Whereupon Mr [Robert] Baldock ordered the jury to find the offender not guilty, it being the father's 50s. & not his two daughters' or hers who had it in possession.[41]
26 [February]: Samuel Gunner of Ashmanhaugh was bound over to the sessions & William Cutting of Beeston St. Lawrence to prosecute him for the extreme beating his prentice child but of 8 years old, who soon after died.[42]
Eodem: John Tod was sent to Bridewell for stealing wood and glorying in it.
3 March: a warrant in order to the making an order about Antingham bastards.[43]
4 [March]: a warrant against Thomas Gambling [of Thwaite, husbandman] & Samuel Bunne [of Colby, labourer] for stealing buck[wheat] in the chaff the last night from Robert Allen of Hanworth [glover] & to search.
Eodem: Thomas Gambling was brought before me & committed. That night 5 [March] he escaped, whereupon I sent out two hues & cries, one to [King's] Lynn etc. & the other to Thetford for the apprehending Gambling & Bunne, being both fled.
6 [March]: Samuel Bunne aforesaid was apprehended & by me sent to the gaol.[44]
10 [March]: a warrant for divers [persons] to testify etc. in Antingham bastard business.[45]
23 [March]: a warrant to remove Rachel Fuller to her master Bassam's in Cromer, being paralytic & a servant.
Eodem: another to provide an house for the widow Pye of Gresham.
27 [March]: a warrant against Samuel Bunne [of Colby, labourer]. He had sold a colt & after took him again by replevin in T. Gambling's name.[46]
28 [March]: a warrant for relief of Philip[pa] Geton of Thurgarton widow.
14 [March]: a warrant with Sir John Palgrave for relief of Margery Nickerson of Aldborough.
18 [March]: a warrant to distrain Duffield, [Harris?] and Gex for Thurgarton poor rate.
22 [March]: a warrant to provide for a poor woman of Alby.
23/24 [March]: John Bond churchwarden & Nicholas Bacon & Christopher Black overseers of Thurgarton to me complained that John Dyball & his wife at our Lady [Day] last came from Roughton where they were last settled as householders for 40 days & more to settle in a new erected cottage in Thurgarton under £10 per annum. And that they are like to be chargeable to Thurgarton. William Spurrell, Robert Risebrough.[47]
25 [March]: a warrant for relief of Mary the wife of Edmund Ashwell of Bradfield.
[25 March]: a warrant against Thomas Knights senior, Thomas Knights junior, William Knights, Samuel Knights, Richard Loveday & Richard Harding for rescuing a distress for chimney money.
[f. 9v] *20 April 1663:* Antingham officers had Sir George Windham's & mine order in the case of the female bastard born by Mary Joyce to which Thomas Simpson was ordered to be the reputed father.

21 [April]: I heard that the said Simpson & Joyce were carried to Aylsham Bridewell to [be] whipped according to that order & our warrant (query).[48]
Eodem: At Holt 46 alehouses were licensed, whereof 14 [were] of our hundred (& 15 unlicensed) & of Holt [hundred] 32 (& [blank] unlicensed) & 7 inns.[49]
27 [April]: a warrant against Robert Herring for departing the service of William Stubs of Alby.
29 [April]: a warrant for relief of the widow Manning of Alby.
30 [April]: Aylmerton appealed from our judgement for settlement of Bouer, his wife, & children & entered recognizance to prosecute the same & send my notice of both to Weybourne under my hand & seal.[50]
2 [May]: a warrant for search in Burrow,[51] Brampton & Stratton Strawless (& where 3 tinkers & a woman with them may be found) for goods of Ann Langtry of Brampton worth £15 stolen out of her house which was broken open.
4 [May]: another warrant & order to pay the widow Manning the 12[d.] a week arrear & 12d. pro futuro.
6 [May]: a warrant of the peace against John Bunnett junior of Aylsham [husbandman] (Judith Smith [wife of Robert, yeoman] of Blickling [was the complainant]).[52]
15 [May]: he did appear before me & was bound.
19 [May]: a warrant for relief of Edward Postle of Roughton.
Eodem: a warrant to convict John Taylor of Trunch, alehousekeeper, for swearing.
20 [May]: a warrant against Bartholomew Bride of Felmingham [yeoman] for beating, turning away & delaying the wages of Robert Batchelour [husbandman] his servant for £7 wages.[53]
21 [May]: a warrant for swearing [William Allison, husbandman] constable of Felmingham.[54]
21° Maii 1663: John Woolsey & John Bond the two churchwardens of Thwaite in the county of Norfolk did complain unto me according to the statute on such behalf late made[55] that Samuel Bunne & his wife (being now great with child) and their child are all poor persons & likely to be chargeable to the parish of Thwaite aforesaid and did on Thursday last being the 14th of this instant come from Colby in the said county where they were last settled (as householders) by the space of forty days & more to settle in a tenement in Thwaite aforesaid under the yearly value of £10 without any agreement of or with the landlord & that the landlord had entered into the lands let formerly with the said tenement and would yesterday have put them out of the possession of the said tenement if he could then have got in. **[f. 10r]** They had Sir John Palgrave's & my warrant to give security or show cause etc.[56]
21 M[ay] 1663: Robert Smith & Judith his wife released the peace against John Bunnett.[57]
28 [May]: a warrant of the peace against Robert Marys [husbandman of Metton] for beating Samuel Smith [labourer] of Metton.[58]
29 [May]: a warrant of the peace against Henry England [of] Honing by Richard England [of] Worstead, his father.
24 April & 5 May: two warrants to remove John Dyball & his wife [poor

persons] from Thurgarton to Roughton.[59]
22 [May]: a warrant for them returning to Thurgarton to show cause. (Till after sessions res[pited?]).[60]
29 [May]: Edward Fox sworn constable of Hanworth instead of Robert Miller.
30 [May]: John Fisher sworn constable of Hanworth instead of Jer. Flaxman.
30 [May]: He was then by my warrant of the same day caused to come before me.
1 Junii: a warrant of the peace against Elizabeth Crow, wife of William Crow of Knapton [husbandman], for threatening Elizabeth Wilton [of same, spinster].[61]
Eodem: George England churchwarden & Edmund Thaxter & Henry Neale (was not present) overseers & Robert Swanne & [blank] Thaxter [all of Bessingham, complained] that William Grey within 40 days now last past did come from Town Barningham where he was an householder to settle in a tenement in Bessingham under £10 per annum contrary to the statute.[62]
Eodem: a warrant against defaulters in highways in Banningham.
Eodem: Edmund & William Thaxters sworn constables of Bessingham.
2 [June]: a warrant of the peace against Richard Morter of North Walsham (David Morter prosecutor).
3 [June]: Thomas Cocke of Beeston licensed by Sir John Palgrave, Sir George Windham & after by myself.
Eodem: William Allison sworn constable of Felmingham.
5 [June]: Anne Lambert of Sheringham licensed by Sir John Palgrave & myself, & T. Cock [was licensed].
8 [June]: a warrant against defaulters in Matlask highways.
9 [June]: a warrant of the peace against Valentine Bullock of Aldborough [tailor] (Richard Bancks [tailor of Hainford] prosecutor).[63]
16 [June]: Richard Ryall sworn constable of Witton, being chose by the homage.
Eodem: Simon Lubbock, a surveyor of Wickmere, had a warrant against defaulters in the [high]ways.
Eodem: a warrant against Matthew Godbold & Margaret his wife for misdemeanours (Robinson of I. [complained]).
17 [June]: a warrant for John Greene to deliver over the town stock & rem. [sic] to the new overseers of Felmingham.
24 [June]: a warrant against George Brook c[onstable?] for abusing the watchmen of Aldborough who set him in stocks.
Eodem: a warrant against Cicely Coxfer for refusing to serve R. Jackson with whom she was hired.
26 [June]: a warrant against Thomas Bun [husbandman], John Smith, Philip Fuller & Frances Riches [spinster] for keeping unlicensed alehouses in Blickling.[64]
Eodem: a warrant against William Grice & Margaret his wife for gaming & disorder in their house; Thomas [Loulman?] prosecutor.
27 [June]: the said Bun by confession & the said Riches by witnesses were convicted & 20s. apiece by my warrant for the same to be levied.[65]

3 [July]: a warrant against Mary King for commonly selling beer in Aylsham, W. Terrell pro[secutor]; to be brought on next Tuesday morning by nine of the clock.[66]
6 [July]: a warrant against Thomas Mileham [woolcomber] for stealing the brick off the church wall of Knapton.[67]
Eodem: a warrant against Samuel Smith, Erasmus Earlham, Samuel Earlham & Jo. Tompson, all of Buxton, for beating John More of Witton because he would not pay all the reckoning.
[f. 10v] *8 Julii 1663:* a warrant against Thomas Howes of Erpingham for beating & drawing blood of William Pull his servant. He gave Pull 8d.[68]
9 [July]: a warrant against defaulters in Marsham highways to make satisfaction.
9 [July]: a warrant against Thomas Corb. [sic] Abraham Moll's servant of Worstead, departing with no cause.[69]
10 [July]: a warrant against William Durrant & Ann his wife for beating & threatening Katherine Green to fire 400 furze [which] migh[t] endanger the firing Aylsham market stead.[70]
14 [July]: a warrant of the peace against Amy the wife of John Streacock, husbandman of Edgefield, upon oath of Armiger Olley, tailor of the same.[71]
20 [July]: a warrant against Francis Lightfoote of Tuttington for departing Crowe's service & carrying away his master's goods.
25 [July]: a warrant against Philip Harvy for departing the service of James Scamler, Esq.
At the sessions at Fakenham [on 23 July 1663], Henry Ampleford appearing, Mr Stileman who was at the cushion said he remembered that about 25 years before there was no inn where his pretended inn now is, whereupon the sessions offered him a licence but he refused to accept one, and they declared & his counsel assented that in case there had been witness he might have been convicted for an unlicensed alehouse. But as to the chief intended question, whether innkeepers might on their own authority without lawful licence commonly sell beer (it being against the letter of the statute & considered together is (in the negative) & very clear), Mr Smith and Mr Pepis being both absent, the court did doubt, but Mr Burleigh said that in Crooke's Report it was agreed that they might.[72]
[f. 11r] *28 Julii 1663:* a warrant to apprehend Samuel Bunne [husbandman] of Thwaite for suspicion of stealing an horse of Mr Richard Hobbys [clerk] of Erpingham.
29º [July]: He was by me sent to the gaol & Mr Hobbys bound to prosecute.[73]
Eodem: John Gunton of Northrepps was convicted by his own confession for keeping an unlicensed alehouse & a warrant [was] granted to levy 20s.
31 Julii: a warrant to apprehend Thomas Corp. [sic] for stealing 12s. 6d. of Abraham Moll in five 2s. 6d. pieces.
Eodem: he was sent to the gaol; Moll [was bound] in £20 to prosecute & a warrant against Jolly to testify.[74]
1 August: Adam Binsly of Beeston, a rogue taken up at Colby with another who had a counterfeit pass & had said that they should have a new pass or be whipped or sent to the gaol and that he had rather be whipped than

go to the gaol, I appointed to be whipped & sent away. The other ran away early this morning.
4 [August]: a warrant against Joseph Smith the runaway apprentice of William Gotts of Briston; it was at large.
7 [August]: a warrant to bring Frances Riches of Blickling [spinster] to be committed to be whipped. She was convicted before me 27 June 1663 for unlicensed alehousekeeping.[75]
15 [August]: 2 warrants of the peace at the desire & oath of Mary, the wife of William Smith of Blickling, against Nicholas Smith of the same & John Prick, apparitor, of Aylsham and also 1 warrant de bone perort [sic] against Francis Balls of Bl[ickling?] for saying that go they to what justice they would he must make the end (it was of the 20s. forfeited by the widow Riches for keeping an unlicensed alehouse) and that he would make it cost the said William Smith (who was constable) 40s. Prick threatened to take a course with the said Mary. Nicholas Smith swore William was cause of his brother's death & Balls said, If you swear it, how shall he help himself.[76]
16 [August]: a warrant of the peace against Henry Spall of Aylsham upon the oath of Mary King, beaten.
17 [August]: [Francis] Balls desired that he might enter the recognizance then because he was to go to his harvest from my house and that William Smith might prove the offence afterward, for he had come without his witnesses. So I had their informations only, without oath, which Smith promised to do.[77]
Eodem: a warrant of Norwood Barningham officers to pay Thomas Bunting 30s. due to him at 2s. the week for keeping Clement Olley a poor child put out at that rate or [blank].
24 [August]: Sir Thomas Rant & myself made an order concerning the 3 Bretts between Thurgarton & Erpingham.[78]
Eodem: Christopher Eastwick [labourer, bound] in £10, Thomas Sharping [yeoman] et John Greene [husbandman] in £5 apiece to keep the peace against Richard Hating [woolcomber]. They were all of Marsham (Mr [Oliver] Neave['s] warrant).[79]
25 [August]: a warrant against William Bower [tailor of Wickmere] for departing the harvest work of Simon Lubbock.[80]
Eodem: a warrant of the peace against Mary, Elizabeth & Grace, three of the daughters of Richard Hating, at the oath of Ursula Eastwick whom they on Sunday last had beaten. The 24 [August] I sent out a warrant against them for to answer such misdemeanours as should be objected by Christopher Eastwick aforesaid.[81]
31 [August]: [a warrant against] Alice Bower, the wife of William Bower of Wickmere, tailor, upon the oath of Ann Scoller, the wife of Robert Scoller of the same [woolcomber].[82]
3 September: a warrant of the peace against Thomas Crow of Sustead, tailor, upon the oath of Peter Macke of Metton (Crow had also beat Mack & his wife).
[f. 11v] *4 September 1663:* a warrant of the peace against Robert Harmer of Gunton, yeoman, upon the oath of Henry Presse, husbandman, whom Harmer had beaten & [after?] he was pulled off him had threatened that

he would run through any of Turner's, Presse's master's, family (except himself), and that he would [have] killed Presse if he had not been pulled off.
10 [September]: a warrant against Anthony Annison and Mary his daughter, whom he violently took out of the service of Richard Austine of Swafield.[83]
19 [September]: a warrant for the relief of Coates of Blickling. He had 6d. for himself & 6d. for a child.
28 [September]: a warrant against [Richard] Grout [husbandman of Northrepps] for stealing [Clement] Doaghty's pears.[84]
Eodem: a warrant against Joan Buttivant for drawing beer in Colby.[85]
29 [September]: a warrant of the peace against Henry Johnsons, upon oath of Valentine Bulluck.
Eodem: a warrant to provide an house for James Purdy of Saxthorpe.
4 8bris: a warrant of the peace against Henry Soame (son of Jo. Soame) upon oath of T. Leasy.
12 October: a warrant against William Bateman [of Southrepps] to pay William Ryall 18s. 6d. for his harvest wages yet due.[86]
15 October: at Walsingham [quarter sessions] I gave the charge.[87]
23 [October]: a warrant for apprehending Robert Driver of Bradfield for stealing 2 neat beasts of John Cheanye's & two others of John Gibbs (both of Stratton Mary)[88] & selling the same to John Austen of Wrentham in Suffolk for £8. To the chief constable. Thomas his son prosecutor.
24 [October]: a warrant to the chief constable, Sustead having no constables, for apprehending Martha Nicholls [widow of Sustead] & Margaret Davy [her sister], the first for stealing with Margaret Whight [alias Margaret Underwood, spinster of Gresham] 3 geese of William Frost's & the second for rescuing her sister, being apprehended.[89]
Eodem: I took the examination of Margaret White & sent her to the gaol.
26 [October]: a warrant against Richard Buttivant for departing the service of his master Colby. Ban[ningham?].
Eodem: I took the examination of Martha Nicholls, & I & Sir John Palgrave bailed both.
28º [October]: a warrant against John Bulman, thaxter, Thomas Bell, tailor, Jeremy Loveday, shoemaker, Thomas Pooly, cooper, & Susan his wife, all of Aylsham, and Thomas Gryme, tailor of Ingworth, to answer misdemeanours etc. to be objected by Katherine Starlinge & others. They had bought a goose of her for 1s. 2d. & when for want of change they pretended they could not pay she gave the 2 first 2 groats, & they paid the reckoning with it & left her unpaid & kept her till near night, & then she was forced to get away at the back door. They gave her 2s. 2d. at Aylsham.
30 [October]: a warrant against John Flaxman for not paying Peter Rodgers his harvest wages [of] 16s. & 7s. for four days' work, being promised & delayed to be paid.
31 [October]: John Cockman sworn constable of Antingham.
2 9bris: a warrant of the peace against William Empson of Aylsham, alehousekeeper, upon the oath of Gregory Hewitt of the same [husbandman] whom he had beaten & threatened because he would not

pay 4d., whereas he had called for no beer. 4 townsmen had then been in his house at play & drinking till two of the clock in the morning, William Hewitt, John Pescod, John Soame & Robert Leaman, who took Empson off Hewitt.[90]

[f. 12r] *9 9bris 1663:* a warrant of the peace against Henry Haylett of Blickling, butcher, upon the oath of Mary Wot [wife of Henry of same]. He had poisoned her dog & threatened her.[91]

Eodem: Thomas White sworn constable of Briston. He saith that the leeters to Mr Howe's manor choose the one constable and that the leeters at Thornage manor choose the other.[92]

12 [November]: a warrant against Christian Tuck [spinster] for keeping an unlicensed alehouse in Antingham St. Margaret's. On the 16th she was convicted before me by the oaths of Thomas Martins [of Antingham] & Rowland Bell.[93]

16 [November]: a warrant against Joan Buttivant of Colby [spinster] for keeping such alehouse.[94]

17 [November]: [I] set my hand to a warrant to remove [blank] a poor man from Sherington to Thursford his last place of residence (being Mr Britif's mean draft [of a warrant]). At sessions it appeared the complaint was not made within the 40 days & that the tenement was [one word illegible].

17 [November]: a warrant of the peace against Thomas Bacon of Dilham, yeoman (a bailiff [of Tunstead hundred]), at the oath of Eleanor Starky, the wife of William Starky of Felmingham, alehousekeeper, whom he had once beaten & twice threatened, & the chief cause was because she would not let him lie with her or her maid when he had sent away her husband to give an appearance upon his summons.[95]

18 [November]: a warrant against William Starky & the abovesaid Eleanor his wife to be brought before me or etc. with sureties for the good abearing. They had beaten Bacon, thrown salt in the bailiffs' eyes & cut their bridles & stirrups & stabbed one of their horses & then came first to complain.[96]

Eodem: Joan Buttivant was convicted by the oaths of William Coxton of Colby & Edmund Tooly of Suffield for selling of beer contrary to law in Colby aforesaid. Whereupon I then granted my warrant to levy 20s. for the poor to the constables of Colby aforesaid.

23 [November]: John Bond & Edmund Hewitt sworn constables of Thwaite; John Black sworn one of the constables of Colby; Edward Crosby sworn constable of Metton.[97]

24 [November]: a warrant against Thomas Leasy of Aylsham [yeoman] for putting away Richard Flatfoote [husbandman] his servant, hired for £7 wages & 12[s.] given in earnest, who had served him 7 weeks of his year, sowed the winter corn & was then put away without any wages etc.[98]

26 [November]: a warrant to apprehend Richard Clerk, a Roughton boy, for stealing 5s. in a box, being the goods of Robert Blofield, gentleman, in Hanworth.[99]

27 [November]: They could not prove anything & the boy denied it, so respited.

[27 November]: Ralph Cooper & John Drake churchwardens of the parish of Roughton (as Drake now tells me) have formerly complained to Sir Thomas Rant, kt., that Anne Matlaske hath within forty days come from

Hanworth where she had been last before settled for 40 days & upwards to settle in a tenement in Roughton under £10 by the year.
[f. 12v] *27⁰ November 1663:* John Drake sworn constable of Roughton.
30 November: Mr Thomas Lewyn one of the churchwardens & William Crowland one of the overseers of the poor of Knapton (John Worth the other churchwarden & overseer there being sick) did complain unto me that Thomas Neave & his wife did within 40 days last past come from Great Yarmouth in this county, where they were last settled for 40 days & above as householders, to settle in a tenement or cottage in Knapton aforesaid under the yearly value of £10 where they be also inmates etc.
Eodem: a warrant against Henry Colby of Thwaite, labourer, for st[ealing?] William Foxe's 3 ducks.
Eodem: a warrant against Robert House of Aylsham for not paying Edmund Rolfe his wages etc.
[7?] December: a general warrant (with Sir John Palgrave) against Henry Harryson of West Beckham for selling an horse to Robert Greene of Walsham for £3 paid & another nag, which horse Hembling his brother-in-law soon after retrieved.
14 [December]: a warrant to search for a piece of sallow[100] & a gate post stolen from Mr Jay.
16 [December]: a general warrant to carry [William] Starky & his wife [Eleanor] to the gaol for want of sureties for their good ab[earing].[101]
22 [December]: a warrant against William Allison [husbandman], one of the constables of Felmingham, who said in the hearing of Robert Fisher [gentleman], the other constable, that I did not do law because I did not take the informations of all parties & would not let the witness that did speak say all he had to say (meaning in a case wherein Bacon & Greene & others had complained against William Starky and his wife).[102]
Eodem: William Starky of Felmingham, alehousekeeper, was convicted before me for permitting Robert Fox of Suffield, carpenter, on the 21st day of this instant December to[103] continue drinking in the alehouse of the said William Starky in Felmingham aforesaid by the space of[104] five hours contrary to the law.
Eodem: the said Robert Fox was then convicted for the continuing tippling in the said alehouse aforesaid. Surety given for Starky & wife's good ab[earing].
24 [December]: I sent John Smith of Blickling [labourer] to Aylsham Bridewell for a month unless he should by my or some other's warrant in the mean[time be released]. He had committed many misdemeanours & drawn beer, being formerly convicted.[105]
Eodem: a warrant against[106] Frances Riches. She being formerly convicted drew beer again & threatens others that speak to her of it.
30 [December]: a warrant to search for a shirt & handkerchief of Martin Bidny of Roughton [husbandman], Dyony Lound, wife of Richard Lound [husbandman] of Northrepps, being seen on Christmas day last to wear an handkerchief for which she gave a suspicious account. 'Twas informed me that about the time these things were stolen, she sold a new shirt of her husband's.[107]
1 Januarii [1664]: I discharged the abovesaid John Smith out of Bridewell.

Eodem: a warrant against Philip Fuller [labourer] for commonly selling beer in Blickling.[108]
4 [January]: a warrant for Peter Abs [oatmealmaker] to be sworn one of the constables of Runton.[109]
6 [January]: a warrant of the peace against John Arborow of Cromer upon the oath of Nicholas Flockden, whom yesternight he had waylaid, knocked down, beaten & threatened.
[f. 13r] *7 ⁰ Januarii 1664:* Peter Abbs was sworn constable of Runton.
Eodem: Philip Fuller was convicted by his own confession before me to have used for a month before commonly selling [sic] beer in Blickling contrary to the statute, whereupon I made my warrant to the churchwardens to levy the 20s.
8⁰ [January]: William House & William Dyball, the two churchwardens & overseers of the poor of the parish of Banningham,[110] did complain unto me that Anne Yell with her two children (being poor persons & likely to be chargeable to the said parish) did on or about the 16th day of December last past come to settle in a tenement in Banningham aforesaid under the yearly value of £10 (being one of their town houses), and that she the said Anne Yell with the eldest of the said children was last legally settled for forty days & above in the parish of St. Augustine in the city of Norwich (where the said eldest child was born) as an householder, and that the youngest child is not above a quarter old & ought to be settled in the said parish of St. Augustine.[111]
9⁰ [January]: a warrant of the peace against Mary the wife of Anthony Garrett of Tuttington upon the oath of Maryan Presse, widow, of the same, whom she hath yesterday threatened to be the death of at one time or other & pursued.
Eodem: a warrant for John Gay of Ingworth to appear before me on Monday by one of the clock, for then the witnesses are to convict him for unlicensed alehousekeeping.
11⁰ [January]: Edmund Chapman & John Browne the two churchwardens of Itteringham did according to the statute complain unto me that Mary Earle, spinster, being a poor person & likely to be chargeable to the parish of Itteringham, did within forty days now last past (that is on or about tomorrow[112] month) come from Wickmere, where she was last settled for forty days & more as a servant,[113] to the said parish[114] of Itteringham and doth yet continue there in the house on [sic] one of the overseers. I made an ordinary warrant to convey her to Wickmere, with another [justice] to be got to join.[115]
Eodem: Bacon & Starky's wife discharged each other.[116]
15 [January]: a warrant against Christopher Person for detaining Joseph Culle's flail & 6d. wages. Ant[ingham?]
Eodem: William Frost [husbandman of Gresham was bound] in £10 & Thomas Buthell [miller of same] in £5 to indict & give evidence against Martha Nichols [spinster of Sustead] & Margaret Whight [spinster of Gresham] for stealing Frost's 3 geese.[117]
19 [January]: Robert Wiggett a poor child of Blickling bound till 24 to Simon Lubbock of Wickmere, his executor & administrators. I set my hand, & they were to go to Sir Thomas Rant for his etc.

[f. 13v] *25 January 1664:* George England the only churchwarden of Bessingham, with Edmund Thaxter & Henry [Whall?], the two[118] overseers there, & William Thaxter, inhabitant there, made complaint that William Elwood within 40 days last past, that is in Christmas last past, did come from Edgefield etc. where he was last settled with his father as his servant, to settle in a tenement in Bessingham aforesaid under the yearly value of £10, where he is an inmate & his rent about 20s. value, being a poor person & likely to be chargeable to the parish of Bessingham aforesaid.
12 [January]: a warrant to search for divers grocery & mercery wares stolen out of the shop of Anthony Greene of Aylsham, grocer, in Burgh, which was last night broke open.
6 February: a warrant to search the house of Valentine Bullock, tailor, in Aldborough, for a spoon & other goods of the Lady Windham, by Jane Jegon her woman suspected to be stolen by Sara Beverly her maid.[119]
8 [February]: a warrant against William Starky of Felmingham to answer to misdemeanours.[120]
Eodem: Richard Lound from Sir John Palgrave desired me to draw up a warrant preparatory for sending back Margery Smith widow & John Fuller late son of John Fuller deceased, being two likely to be chargeable etc., who on Thursday last was five weeks came from Buxton in this county to settle (with her son) in [a] tenement in Gresham under the yearly rent of £10 per annum, vizt. of £3, the complaint being this day duly made to Sir John by Richard Fuller & James Money, the churchwardens of Gresham aforesaid.
Eodem: a warrant to search for wools & other things stolen from the Lady Windham.
Eodem: & another for apprehending Sara Beverley & Edmund Henery of Aldborough for the stealing of goods of the Lady Windham at Uffords.[121]
11 [February]: I set hand to Sir John Palgrave's warrant to pay Humfrye's wife the 11s. arrear of his collection & thenceforth 3s. by the week or [else] his 12d. to continue with allowance of firing and house rent.
12 [February]: a warrant general against Mary Dove & Elizabeth Dove of North Walsham, spinsters, who have taken a featherbed & other things from Prudence Boyard of the same.
1º Marchii: a warrant for John Bacon & Robert Risbrough to appear before me etc.
3 [March]: they appeared & were each sworn constables of Thurgarton.[122]
13 [March]: a warrant against Nicholas Maryall to answer to what shall be objected by Richard Ransome, clerk, & his master. He was drunk & threatened to kill his master.
18 [March]: a warrant to the churchwardens & overseers of Barningham Parva to provide Mary Townshend & Stephen her husband an habitation for their money.
[f. 14r] *[18 March]:* a warrant to provide an habitation for [blank] upon the engagement of their mothers for the farm, he being under age.
21 [March]: a warrant to provide firing & give a weekly allowance unto Godfrey Moone of Banningham, being a poor sick man & one upon whom Yell's wife & two children have been put, whereby his firing is spent.[123]
30 [March]: a warrant of misdemeanour against Christopher Perkins at

[blank] Moyses's complaint.
1 April: a warrant to apprehend Thomas Cubitt for getting Margaret White with child.[124]
Eodem: a warrant of the peace against him on[125] the oath of Robert Underwood.
18 Marchii: a warrant against John Greene [the younger, bricklayer] for keeping an unlicensed alehouse in Aylsham, who was convicted 23 March upon oath of 2 witnesses. And 20s. to be by my warrant levied.[126]
2 April: a warrant against Robert Riches of Aylsham for unlicensed selling of beer. To appear on Thursday next at my house.
Eodem: a warrant to apprehend Thomas Yell, who the Monday following was brought before me and sent to the gaol for an incorrigible or dangerous rogue, & Mr Philip Jay & Simon Starling were bound to indict & prosecute.
Eodem: a warrant general against John Webster of Northrepps, who found Pull's tools.
[Eodem]: a general warrant against William [blank] for breaking ope the doors of [blank] of Aylsham.
Eodem: a warrant against William Pull for departing the service of Dennis Venner of Cromer his master, his time not being out till Michaelmas.
9 [April]: a warrant to apprehend one Thomas or William Bedingfield & another person, who are both in the warrant particularly described, who pretend themselves seamen & had a pass pretended from me & Sir John Palgrave for Boston, who are suspected on the first of this month in the morning to have stolen the black horse & the saddle & ring halter of William Stubs of Alby, and[127] did then break down the pave of the wall to have got out a mare of Stubs that was locked up. And [they] were tracked thence through Calthorpe & Wolterton, where Mr Bacon is said to have then lost £4 worth of linen, and thence through Lubbock of Wickmere his yard and so towards Fakenham.
12 [April]: a general warrant against Jezebel Purgall of Southrepps [widow] for beating & threatening to kill Henry Allen of the same.
13 [April]: a warrant of the peace against the said Jezebel upon oath of Miles Purgall [husbandman of Southrepps].
14 [April]: she appeared before me & by her, the constables' & the neighbours' relations she had had the wrong, and Allen & Purgall had beaten & bruised her.[128]
[f. 14v] *25 April 1664:* Joseph Riches of Swanton Abbot, miller, was bound to his majesty in £10, & Thomas Morly & Robert Brand both of the same town, worsted weavers, in £5 apiece, upon condition that the said Riches should personally appear at the next quarter sessions at Norwich and in the meantime should keep the peace etc. chiefly toward Elizabeth Slater of the same town [singlewoman]. She is his wife's sister & had before Mr [Jacob] Preston sworn etc.[129]
26 [April]: a warrant against [Giles] Sprunt [labourer of Skeyton] for departing the service of Robert Harmer [yeoman] of Gunton.[130]
Eodem: a warrant for the new chosen constables of Felbrigg to be sworn.[131]
Eodem: a general warrant against Cleare Salmon of Antingham, butcher, for beating Richard Cully his servant (because he would not accuse the apprentice for kissing Salmon's wife while he was stepped aside).

27 [April]: Richard Allen & Dennis Flaxman were sworn constables of Felbrigg.
2 Maii: a warrant against Peter Rodgers [labourer of Sustead] for sawing & breaking a gate of Mr [Thomas] Blofield [gentleman].
Eodem: he confessed the same before me & I ordered Mr Blofield 2s. which Rodgers paid.[132]
4 [May]: a warrant against Thomas Leasy for not paying John Moyses his late servant 17s. 6d. of his wages due at Our Lady & for the week after till he fell sick.
5⁰ [May]: John Cullee & Thomas Goulder, the two churchwardens of Trunch in this county, did make complaint unto me that Joseph Rump within 40 days last past (that is about three weeks last past) did come from Felmingham in this county where he was last settled as a servant for 40 days & more (that is, for about the space of a year) to settle in a tenement in Trunch aforesaid under the yearly value of £10, that is of about 16s. per annum. And that he then was & yet is a poor person & likely to be chargeable to the parish of Trunch aforesaid and therefore prayed that the said parish might be by good security discharged of him or that otherwise he might be removed back to Felmingham aforesaid according to the law. We gave Wednesday in Whitsunweek by 2 in the afternoon for our judgements.
Eodem: a warrant to apprehend Samuel Bunne [labourer of Alby] for stealing a cart rope of John Bennington's [yeoman of Alby] (which Bun had sold young Timothy Puxly for 2s. & he the same day [sold it] to young Thomas Empson for 2s. 6d.), & old [John] Puxly [roper of Erpingham] had at first sold [it to] Bennington.[133]
9⁰ [May]: a warrant against Richard Shale [tailor] of Paston for suspicion of stealing a lamb sold amongst others by William Austine to Richard Fennant, both of the same.[134]
11 [May]: a general warrant against Robert Underwood of Gresham for beating & threatening to kill Elizabeth his wife.[135]
[f. 15r] *13⁰ Maii:* a warrant to bring Peter Lennow of Mattishall cum Burrow, woolcomber, then being at Calthorpe, to be examined concerning a bastard laid to him by Frances Margetson [spinster] of Blickling & to bring sureties for his forthcoming etc. & good behaviour in the meantime.
Eodem: he came, denied the charge, had no sureties, so sent to the gaol.[136]
Eodem: a warrant against defaulters in Aldborough highways.
14⁰ [May]: a general warrant against Elizabeth, wife of Robert Underwood, & Prudence Pye. They took away divers goods & 5s. 3d. in money from Margaret White.
17⁰ [May]: a general warrant against Edmund Maris of Southrepps, blacksmith, for tippling against the will of Unica Risbrough [of same] & abusing of her.[137]
Eodem: a general warrant against John Gardner, seaman, for drawing a knife & cutting the wrist of Alice Crowne; the quarrel was about stone.
18⁰ [May]: a general warrant against Rose Neave (Woodrowe's servant) for beating of An Py, Prudence Pye, Underwood's [servant] & Katherine Dobson Mrs. White's servant.
19⁰ [May]: a general warrant against Robert Underwood [of Gresham,

bailiff] & Elizabeth his wife & another eodem against Crow of Sustead (for beating Thomas Copeman [of Thurgarton, labourer]).[138]
[Eodem]: Rose Neave gave An Py 12d. for her satisfaction.
20 [May]: Underwood forgave Copeman what he owed & gave him 18d. & Copeman is to come no more at Underwood's. And they, Thaxter & Carvell are to be mutually against each other (except such debt as Carvell oweth to Underwood).
Eodem: a warrant to Cromer officers to provide Pull an house for his dwelling, his father engaging etc.
Eodem: a warrant of the peace against Sara Hooke, the wife of Edmund Hooke of Sheringham, seaman, upon the oath of Cecily Dixon, the wife of Edmund Dixon of the same, pedder. Hooke had put Dixon into the court.
21 [May]: Hooke was to take Dixon out of the court & Dixon to pay for the peace.
Eodem: a warrant for William Fiddiman & Robert Cooke to be sworn constables of Sheringham.[139]
23 [May]: a general warrant against Edmund Bell of Thurgarton [labourer] for beating his wife.[140]
[n.d.]: two warrants against defaulters in Aldborough & Wickmere highway days.
31 [May]: a warrant against John Herring of Colby, labourer, for keeping there an unlicensed alehouse. Joan Buttivant now wife of the said John was the 18th day of the last November convicted before me for the like & 20s. was levied of her goods. And now she brags that when her husband be gone into Marshland she will draw beer again in despite of the townsmen.
[f. 15v] *31 Maii 1664:* a warrant of the peace against Thomas Newland of Knapton, carpenter, upon the oath of William Landsdale of North Walsham, feltmaker, whom he had without cause beaten, bruised and threatened.[141]
Eodem: upon oath of William Barne & William Callow both of Colby aforesaid, John Herring was convicted for using to sell beer in Colby of his own authority, not being thereto lawfully licensed. And the said John then confessed that he had had three barrels & two barrels of beer of William Tirrell of Aylsham & that he also lately had two barrels of beer more of [blank] Harlo of Southrepps and that five of them be sold out and the sixth now in drawing. And I granted then my warrant to levy the 20s.
Eodem: a warrant general against Robert Watson [labourer of Thwaite] for misusing & threatening Em Kid widow [of Alby].[142]
1 [June]: a warrant for witnesses to testify in a case to be brought before me.
2 [June]: a general warrant against Mary the wife of John Clerke & Dorothy the wife of John Priest, both of Weybourne, to answer Elizabeth Cooper of the same.
4 [June]: a warrant against Susan Tompson [spinster, widow of John Tompson] for misbehaviour towards John Gunton her son-in-law [husbandman], both of Northrepps.[143]
13 [June]: a warrant for George England & Guybon Linne to be sworn

constables of Bessingham, being fit persons & next to the said office.
Eodem: a general warrant against the wife of Thomas Wegg of Saxthorpe. She had three chickens, two of James Lacon's of Oulton & the other of his neighbour's which Lacon saw, & they & three more were said to be stolen by an unknown person after Thursday evening & sold on Friday morning to Weg's wife as she saith, but those first three.
15 [June]: Guybon Lynne sworn constable of Bessingham instead of Edmund Thaxter.
14 & 16 [June]: 2 warrants for highway defaulters, one for Hempstead the other for Plumstead.
16 [June]: a general warrant against Robert Some for throwing Mary Thorpe & Margaret Bockinge off their horse, whereby Mary had her wrist put out of joint & Margaret is so ill being bruised that there is danger of her life (though they prayed him to forbear, he having once before thrown the said Mary off of her horse).
17 [June]: 2 warrants against defaulters in highways, in Wickmere general & Metton special.
18 [June]: a general warrant against Mathew Cooper, an apprentice of John Harris of Erpingham [blacksmith], for divers miscarriages & threatening to run away.[144]
[f. 16r] *22 Junii 1664:* a general warrant against Elizabeth Catton wife of Thomas Catton, labourer, Margaret Tyler & Mary Crow, spinsters, & all of Southrepps. They had threatened to stab Nicholas Smith the bailiff.
23 [June]: a warrant of the peace against Bevill Skelton of Suffield Esq. & William Morgan of the same [gentleman], now or late servant of the said Bevill Skelton.[145]
24 [June]: a warrant against William Clemens, a carpenter of Worstead, for beating & bruising Peter Peeke of Witton, joiner (then in work with him), so as he is in danger of his life, having lain by it these 14 days & not being able so much as to turn him in his bed notwithstanding the means used. See 29 [June].
Eodem: Richard Whitaker & William Ryall sworn constables of Aldborough.
27 [June]: a warrant of the peace against Cicely Key, wife of Thomas Key of Bacton Parva cum Keswick, worsted weaver, upon the oath of Susan Allison of Bromewell, spinster.[146]
Eodem: a warrant against Robert Swan for departing the service of Robert Swan [carpenter] of Southrepps, his master, the term of his apprenticeship not yet out by near two years.[147]
Eodem: a general warrant against Thomas Copeman [labourer] who had beaten his wife [Elizabeth] extremely.[148]
29 [June]: a warrant against Thomas Cooke & Robert Jennys, the old overseers [of Sheringham], to clear their account against divers exceptions therein, amounting to 13s. 4d., & 4d. for a warrant.[149]
Eodem: Robert Cooke sworn one of the constables of Sheringham instead of Edmund Greene.
[Eodem]: Thomas Smith one of the constables of Worstead informed me that Clemens & Peeke are agreed & that Clemens gave Peeke 13s. 4d. See 24 [June].

Eodem: a warrant for Daniel Lynes, servant to James Smith of Worstead, butcher, for departing his service, his [time] being not to expire till about Michaelmas next & to show good cause.
[n.d.]: I made an end between the Swans, that the prentice should work with his master till his time should expire, give his mistress 40s., & that his master should let him have his earnings & give [him] his clothes, linen, & woolen presently & an axe or belt at the end of his time. See 27 [June].
5 Julii: a warrant of the peace against Mary the wife of Richard Shale of Paston, tailor, upon the oath of Robert Colker [labourer] of the same, whom she threat to knock on the head.[150]
Eodem: John Flaxman & Edmund Barnes, the two overseers of the poor of Tuttington, made complaint unto me that Elizabeth the wife of [blank] Shepheard of Pockthorpe in the city of Norwich, tinker or metal man, did about 3 weeks now last past come with Elizabeth Kitchin & Philip Kitchin, two of her children by[151] William Kitchin her former husband, to Tuttington and did leave the said two children there with the wife of Ralph Lightfoote who keepeth scholars, pretending **[f. 16v]** *Julii 5⁰ 1664* that she would come again in two or three days & take them away but since did never come. And [the overseers] did also then inform me that the said Ralph was yesterday at Pockthorpe to have spake with the said Shepheard & his wife and could not hear of either of them there. Whereupon they conclude that the said Shepheard & his wife are travelled the country or live somewhere obscured and that the said two children, in regard Lightfoote will no longer keep them, must become their towncharge. For preventing whereof they have made this complaint & desired that the said two children may be removed to Pockthorpe where Shepheard, his wife & the said two children were last settled for three years or thereabouts. They say the two children were both born at Aylsham and that the house of the said Lightfoote is worth but 40s. per annum or thereabouts.[152]
6 & 4 [July] ante: William Lansdale [feltmaker of North Walsham] relaxavit Thomas Newland [carpenter of Knapton], & Elizabeth Slayter [spinster of North Walsham, late of Swanton Abbot, released] Joseph Riches [miller of Swanton Abbot].[153]
6 [July]: a general warrant at large against Robert Rix [husbandman] & Sara Cley, both of Worstead. Samuel Tuck informs me that Sara is 22 weeks gone with child & that she chargeth Rix for the reputed father, who pretends Robert Tuck, whose house she keepeth, is its father & hath threatened that if she lay the child to him the said Rix he will slit her nose. But formerly[154] (after he was out of his apprenticeship with the said Robert Tuck) he hath bragged that he had had the use of her body and might when he listed.
7 [July]: Sara Cley charged Robert Rix to be the father of the child she is now with, & he freely acknowledged as much, so [I] sent him to the gaol in regard he had no sureties etc., which he I believe will get. Done 8 July.[155]
Eodem: a warrant of the peace against Margaret Smith of Blickling, widow, James Smith her son, & Ann Smith her daughter. The next day they agreed, 2s. given.[156]
8⁰ [July]:[157] I granted the warrant to remove the Kitchins to Pockthorpe, but I especially charged John Flaxman to get another justice's hand unto it of the quorum.[158]

Eodem: Robert Rix [was bound] in £20, Luke Metcalfe in £10, & Rich Craskfield in £10 for Rix his appearance at Michaelmas sessions at the shirehouse & for his good behaviour in the meantime.[159]
10 [July]: a warrant of the peace against Edmund Hooke of Sheringham, seaman, upon the oath of Alice Cooper [widow], whom Hooke's wife had beaten on Friday last & the said Hooke had extremely beaten & threatened also yesterday.[160]
[f. 17r] *11 [July]:* a warrant of the peace against Daniel Durrant of North Walsham, labourer, upon the oath of Mary Bawcock of the same, a maid whom he grossly abused by words & struck & dazzled her & tore her waistcoat & pursued her with the slings, swearing he would knock her on the head & that only because she had seriously reproved him for swearing and banning.
Eodem: a warrant against Robert Burton, the apprentice of Robert Neave of Paston, for departing the service of his mistress two years & near an half before his term end.[161]
13⁰ [July]: I was at Norwich general quarter sessions, where Mr Bacon had the cushion, as Mr Long had before him & Mr Corey & Mr Baldock were to have after him,[162] where I learnt that one bound to the peace but a fortnight before the sessions is to be continued (that is, bound again to the next) because till then 'tis thought the blood will not well be cooled. And that if the party threaten to sue the other & not leave him worth a 4d., they hold it a good cause to continue etc. him.
Eodem: Robert Fisher of Felmingham having been suspected to have held correspondency with the rebels in the north was bound to these sessions & upon his appearance 'twas moved that some of the bench would go apart & hear & examine the matter & make report back to the court. And after, that I would do it, which I offered to do with Mr Baldock or some other. Sir William Doyly,[163] Sir Thomas Rant & myself went and upon information upon oath of Ann Simpson of North Walsham it did appear to us that Robert Fisher had got his servant with child & for concealment thereof, about last Candlemas was two years, she was by Thomas Simpson conveyed from Norwich, whither she had first been removed, to his brother's in Yorkshire, where she was delivered. They were to have gone on foot had not Simpson bought an horse for 38s. to carry her or both. And about a month after, she & her child were brought back again by Simpson & the child put to nurse at one Walter Marveyl's in King's Lynn (for the town's[164] indemnity Fisher & Simpson gave security in £40) where it died soon after. Simpson, who had formerly been of the parliament's army, was observed to be intimate with Fisher and that they carried the business with great secrecy, so as nothing appeared but the [secrecy?] abovesaid, & that Simpson who owed Mr Cooke money gave a letter of attorney to Mr Cooke to receive & recover whatsoever Fisher owed Simpson. And Simpson near his death told the matter to the informant and that Fisher yet owed him £5. She [Ann Simpson] after her husband's death had 2s. 6d. given her by Fisher, who promised her the rest in time but withal told her that if she discovered it to any or to Mr Thomas Lewyn in particular she should have nothing. And she told thereof much to others & to Lewyn that 'twas £3.[165]

[f. 17v] *14 Julii 1664:* a warrant for John Harper [brickmaker] chosen at the leet 12 July predicto to be sworn constable of Trunch.
16 [July]: he was by me sworn constable there instead of Thomas Primrose.[166]
18 [July]: a warrant against Sara (wife of Edmund Hooke seaman), Cecily Leeds, widow, & Elizabeth (the wife of William Grice, husbandman), all of Sheringham, for stealing last night the green pease of Thomas Cooke the elder growing in his close. They sell pease for 2d. the peck & give of them to their swine.[167]
24 [July]: a warrant of the peace against Mary Holmes the wife of Daniel Holmes now or late of Ony in Buckinghamshire, a musicianer, upon the oath of Elizabeth Kirby of North Walsham, whom the said Mary threatened to kill etc.
Eodem: a warrant of the peace against William now or late footboy, footman or servant of Bevill Skelton Esq. [of Suffield], upon the oath of Nicholas Smith [husbandman of Gresham].[168]
Eodem: a warrant of the peace against Edmund Marys of Southrepps, blacksmith, upon the oath of James Diball, Mr Greye's man & Goodwife Risbroughe's son-in-law. He desired to come into Diball's room, & Diball desiring him to forbear because he was his enemy, Maris thereupon fell upon Diball & drew blood.
27 [July]: Richard Clerk of Roughton bound apprentice with Ralph Cooper of the same till his age of 24 years. Sir Thomas Rant was to join.
28 [July]: a general warrant against Thomas Starky, labourer, William Starky his son, now or late alehousekeeper, Eleanor his wife and Erasmus Earlin, tailor & her brother [all of Felmingham], (who for ought I saw) had the 26th of this July robbed Katherine Dobson of Gresham coming home from the fair at Southrepps about half a mile from the fair of her hat, her scarf, her handkerchief & all her money being 1s. 10d. and threatened to strip her, & the said Thomas did after beat & bruise her.[169]
29 [July]: All save Earlum appeared and the truth appeared to me to be [that] Dobson had carried herself loosely with Earlum[170] & others in Starkye's booth & she went thence, leaving 4d. to pay for her breakfast after she had been asked for Starkye's hatchet (which she said she saw on the church wall & was after all this there again found). Starky & another went after her & perceiving Earlhum leading her by the hand, Starky sent back the other for the rest, who came & saw Earlum carnally lie with her in a fur[ze] close with all their parts under their waists naked save where her apron covered his hips. Whereupon they took the handkerchief, scarf & hat and brought them both to the constable, who would not meddle with them. And now they brought the things & delivered them to her, and she paid the 4d., & the money, which was but 19d., she gave Earlum to make a composition, who offered his coat.
[f. 18r] *30 Julii 1664:* a warrant of the peace against Mary Shale the wife of Richard Shale of Paston, tailor, upon the oath of Margaret Empson, wife of John Empson of the same, who[m] she had threatened to knock on the head (& her children).[171]
3º August: a warrant of the peace against John Rymer of Aylsham, cordwainer, upon the oath of Laurence Archer whom he had stook [sic] & threatened.[172]

4 August: I gave the charge at Fakenham sessions, being my third charge in course & second there. I began my charge at the last paragraph (at All this county).[173] The chief observables were one against whom an order was made as father to a bastard, [who] appeared & freely acknowledged that he had had notice of the said order & had refused to obey it. Whereupon I committed him according to the statute. Whereat the justices were at first all dissatisfied, whereupon the statute was read & the business debated & at last by the justices agreed. (But Mr [William] Burleigh, Mr Ward, & young [Nathaniel] Shouldham, being lawyers, said Crooke's Car [sic] was against it, saying it must be the sessions next after the order.[174] Whereas we agreed it must be the next sessions after the entering the recognizance or finding surety. But Shouldham held further that the sessions by 3 Charles I c. 4 must do all or none. But I hold they may do any part, & the commitment upon refusal is left at large & may be by any justice or session.) But after, it appeared that this man was the Bridewellman's prisoner for debt, so it may be queried whether it will be an escape. And I could not commit him to the Bridewellman's prison because that is only a prison to a liberty & not the common gaol.
The next [case] was upon a settlement & was thus: a servant in A married a wife in B, who had a demise of a house in B for a year. Then the servant's time expire & after he comes to the said house in B. He was settled in A half a year & she in B six weeks before the marriage, and the complaint was not made till he came to settle in B. I & 4 others (vidzt. Sir Nicholas L'Estrange, Sir Edward Walpole, Mr Roger Spelman & Mr [Henry] Clifton) settled them in B, but Sir Thomas Guybon & Mr Nathaniel Shouldham, who had removed them to A, & Mr [Samuel] Harsnett & Mr [Nicholas] Stileman, who had another like case to free Snettisham, were against us, upon the general [rule] that a woman is to be settled with her husband.[175] Which so we agreed, that if the woman had been only native, sojourner or servant in B, or the complaint had been within 40 days after she came to B, she should have been sent to her husband in A. But I think if he had been settled without complaint in an house he holds by lease in A, & she had been so settled in an house in B, that there after marriage they may settle in either.
And a goose stealer was convicted & to be whipped.
[f. 18v] *1664* We after a long debate concerning a woman who could get no house (because ill-conditioned), though she was able & willing to pay for it and had laid all summer in a barn, did at last order the overseer then present that she should be permitted to enjoy an house she had contracted & given earnest for till Michaelmas & had gone into but that he opposed it according to the contract, & to provide for her at Michaelmas or from the present elsewhere. And [we] did agree, where we found in such cases officers obstinate, to bind them to the good behaviour, & lastly we gave order for the gaoler for to [have?] 13s. 4d. to carry 2 prisoners to his gaol, we being informed by Mr Carter that it was usual.[176]
6 August: a general warrant against Thomas Pooly & his wife. He & she have scandalously termed & reproached Christian Rust[177] for a bastard-bearing whore & saying Mrs Goodale (they being all of Aylsham) healed a milk sore in her breast (whereas she saith the sore was occasioned by

a fall off an horse when she went to [Great] Yarmouth to her brother then going for [illegible].
9 [August]: a general warrant against the three daughters of the widow Coxfer of Thwaite who had taken away the glean of Samuel Bun's wife & then beat her.
10 [August]: Sir John Palgrave & myself took the informations against & examination of Elizabeth Palmer of Kelling.[178]
16 [August]: a general warrant against Ambrose Cutting [yeoman] of Bacton who had beat Ann Ber [wife of John Ber of Ingworth] going into his close to glean & bid her go to the justice to complain.[179]
23°[August]: Nicholas Pescod & Richard Gouldale the two overseers of the poor of the parish of Colby made complaint unto me that Elizabeth Newman (one of the daughters of Mr Gilbert Parker late of Aldborough) & the wife of one [blank] Newman now living in the kingdom of Ireland, did with her child, being a girl of about 3 or 4 years old, come[180] the last week (& as they conceive the last Friday or Saturday) to settle with Mrs Ann Warren, widow, in Colby aforesaid, but [they do not know] whether as sojourner or by herself for some part of her[181] house, being[182] a tenement in Colby aforesaid under the yearly value of £10. And they fear she hath another child in this country, which with herself & child first abovesaid may become chargeable to the parish of Colby aforesaid, she having been about in this country & having found that neither any place will receive her [n]or her mother now living in Itteringham will or can relieve her.
[f. 19r] *26 [August]:* a general warrant against [Thomas] Grime [tailor] of Ingworth who had frequently abused the widow [Margaret] Welles & cut her pigs' ropes etc.[183]
27 [August]: a general warrant against 4 women of Thorpe [Market] who beat Matlaske's wife of Roughton gleaning in Thorpe where Thorpe poor had refused.
29 [August]: a warrant of the peace against John Rooke of Swafield & Margaret his wife upon the oath of Mary Helsden, wife of Jeremy Helsden of the same, tailor.
Eodem: a warrant of the good behaviour granted against Thomas Gryme first abovesaid who would not, according as he was by Winnow the constable in his majesty's name required, come before me but threatened to sue those who should come before me to inform against him. See their depositions upon oath upon the warrant aforesaid returned then to me by Winnow.[184]
Eodem: a warrant against Elizabeth Allison who had stolen the sheet of Robert Larwood of Aylsham & given part thereof to bury a child in.
30 [August]: a warrant which Thomas Townshend[185] had wrote & signed & sealed for removing of Elizabeth Newman from Colby (who complained to me 23 August predicto) to Witton. He had wrote it for Oliver Neave to have joined.
1 September: Thomas Gryme abovesaid & Henry Gryme of Cawston his brother & Francis Walls of Blickling (bound in £10 & £5 apiece) for the good behaviour of the said Thomas towards etc. & especially to the widow Wellons etc.[186]
Eodem: a warrant of the peace against Robert Underwood of Gresham,

gentleman, upon the oath of Peter Mack of Metton whom he hath threat to be provided for both in his hand & pocket, saying further he must be hanged & as good soon as sine [sic] or for him as another.[187]
5 [September]: a general warrant against William Woolsey & Elizabeth Flockden his daughter. He had beat & he had threatened Margaret Boyce & her sister.
9 [September]: a general warrant against Edmund Tooly [labourer of Suffield] & Ann his wife. She had stolen meal of William Fisher's, which Margaret his wife having spake of [sic] & Tooly threatens suit.[188]
5 & 9 [September]: a warrant for petty sessions to be held at Holt 20 September, at Sustead 21 [September] & Cromer the 23rd (our hundred had two warrants).
Eodem: Mr [Robert] Underwood [gentleman of Gresham] was bound by Sir John Palgrave & Mr [Thomas] Cubitt [gentleman of Metton] & Robert Marys [yeoman of same] by me.[189]
15 [September]: The said Ann Tooley sent to the gaol for the stealing about a quart of wheat meal of the goods of the said William Fisher's.
13 [September]: a warrant for the old overseers of Aylsham to make up their account & to pay in the arrear to the new [overseers] on or by Friday following.
[f. 19v] *17 [September] 1664:* a general warrant against William Crispe, 14, John Collings, 15, & Edmund Watling, 16 or 17, all boys of Cromer, for stealing the Lady Windham's wood. Query, whether felled.
19 [September]: a warrant to search the houses of Samuel Bunne & Daniel Dobs for 16 geese stolen last night from Henry Colby of Thwaite.
Eodem: a warrant for Joseph Dawes to be sworn constable of Hanworth.
Eodem: the said Dawes appeared & was sworn.
Eodem: a warrant general against Mathew Cooper, the runaway prentice of John Harris [blacksmith of Erpingham].[190]
24 [September]: a warrant to the churchwardens & overseers of Bradfield for the relief of John Pattrick & his wife, being old, with the arrears to pay their landlord 10s. to provide them another habitation & allow them weekly what with their work will maintain them.
29 [September]: a warrant for Ann Chapman of Runton to Bridewell at Aylsham. She had stolen 1 dozen ½ yarn from Peter Abs & sold it as she said for 17d. the dozen at Kelling fair, & Abs had let her have an horse thither.[191]
Eodem: a warrant to search in Runton for sacks & other goods lately stolen from Peter Abs of the same.
20 7bris: Samuel Yaxley de Weybourne & John Yaxley de eadem, cordwainer, cognomina seperatim [sic] debere domino regi £20 etc. Conditioned for their appearance at the next general quarter sessions at Walsingham & for their good behaviour in the meantime.
23 [September]: Sir Thomas Rant & myself bailed Tooley's wife. [We bound] him in £10, John Wetherby [of] Suffield & Thomas White of Antingham in £5 apiece.[192]
21 [September]: Elizabeth Annison was bound to the peace, John her husband in £10, John Prick & John Gedney all of Aylsham in £5 apiece, upon my cousin [Francis] Corye's warrant.[193]

30 [September]: a warrant for Henry Soame of Aylsham to pay Edmund Rust 33s. 9d. remainder of his wages, or to be brought etc. to answer the neglect or refusal.
4 8bris: I set my hand to a warrant drawn by Sir John Palgrave for East Beckham overseers to pay the house rent & lay in firing of & to the widow Cley who is aged & [her] daughter impotent.
5 [October]: a general warrant against Cecily Hooke of Sheringham, widow, who had beaten sorely Francis Dixon, so as Edmund his father say he is in danger of his life.[194]
8 [October]: a warrant against Henry Soame for not paying up his man Rust 3s. 9d. wages.
Eodem: a general warrant against the same Soame & Ann his wife for beating George Grout & not paying him his wages & for brick making & delivering at 4s. 6d. per thousand.
3 [October]: a general warrant against William Pull & Sara his wife. She was one was accused 29 September by Ann Chapman (who I sent to Bridewell having conveyed away & sold yarn of [blank] Abbs) for counselling her & for throwing malt into the **[f. 20r]** swilling tub to prevent a search for stolen goods, the said Ann Chapman having told[195] her search would be made upon my warrant granted Abbs 29 September to search.[196]
10 September [sic]: a warrant to convey Susan Spurrell to Bridewell during her distemper but she was not to be corrected.
Eodem: a general warrant against Thomas Hewitt, weaver, who had refused to assist the constable of Aylsham, being duly required to look to a prisoner.
11 [October]: a general warrant against Martha Hay, spinster, the wife of Robert Hay of Cromer, seaman, who is suspected to have stolen two ewe lambs of Robert Sillis, the son of John Sillis and Margaret his wife.[197]
12 [October]: Robert Doughty Esq. & John Durrant, gentleman, the two churchwardens of Aylsham [and] John Coulson & Thomas Risburgh who serves there as overseer for William Car. [sic], did according to the statute complain to me that William Harmer, his wife & child, being poor persons & likely to be chargeable to the town of Aylsham, did since Michaelmas now last past come from Wiveton in this county where he the said Harmer had been settled as an householder for more than forty days before, to settle in Aylsham aforesaid in a tenement there under the yearly value of £10 (vizt. of £3 or £4 or £7 at most).
Eodem: And that Henry Wiggott being a poor person & likely to be chargeable to the said town of Aylsham, did about Michaelmas aforesaid come from Blickling in the said county, where he was settled as a servant for forty days next before & more, to settle in Aylsham aforesaid in a tenement there under the yearly value of £10, vidzt. 20s. per annum or thereabouts, & hath married a wife, being a single person of Aylsham.
Eodem: And that Winifred Bray, the daughter of [blank] Bray of Aylsham, widow, being a person likely to be chargeable to the said town of Aylsham, did within forty days last past come from Knapton in this county where she had been last before settled as [blank] to settle with her said mother in a tenement in Aylsham aforesaid under the yearly value of £10 per annum (vidz. of 20s. or thereabouts).

Eodem: warrants for removing Harmer & Wiggott unless etc.
Eodem: a warrant against Edward Jex to pay Richard Sadler's mother the 33s. remainder of his wages due from Jex, who had served the brick man so long as he had work.
17º [October]: Simon Lubbock & Thomas Flockden sworn the new constables of Wickmere.
19 [October]: a warrant of the peace against Robert Underwood upon the oath of Peter Mackh: Underwood did arrest Mack at the sessions & on Monday last threatened to make him lame all days of his life.
[f. 20v] *21 8bris 1664:* a general warrant against William Elwood of Bessingham, labourer, who was bound to the assizes & good behaviour in the meantime for having almost killed William Ellys of West Beckham, so as he never since spake & is now so paraleptic [sic] as he hath lost the use of his right arm, for glorying in his fact & threatening to run away. It was not proved.[198]
21 [October]: a warrant of the peace against William Turrell of Aylsham upon the oath of Alice the wife of Thomas Smith of Aylsham, husbandman.
Memorandum: Christopher Perkins did by H. Gunton pay my clerk for Robert Moyses his late servant 24s. So I perceive he will have a back reckoning with his man.
24 [October]: William Turrell bound: he saith the woman first struck him & that they have have [sic] endamaged him by swine, that that night he had an hog worth 4 nobles stabbed, so as he was fained to carry his swine home in a cart.
24 [October]: a warrant of the good behaviour against Jeremy Loveday, husbandman, who hath got Alice Slaughter of spinster [sic] with child, both of Aylsham.[199]
26 [October]: John Springwell sworn constable of Wolterton.[200]
27 [October]: Richard Leonard sworn constable of Overstrand.[201]
Eodem: Christopher Cooper & Edmund Clerke, the two churchwardens of the parish of Sheringham, did according to the statute complain unto me that John Todd, his wife & four children did within 40 days last past (that is, at Michaelmas last past) come[202] from Edgefield in this county where they were last before settled forty days & more, & he the said John Todd as an housekeeper, to settle in a tenement in Sheringham aforesaid[203] under the yearly value of £10 per annum (that is of 40s. by the year or thereabouts). And that the said John Todd, his wife & four children are poor persons & likely to be chargeable to the said parish of Sheringham, and [the churchwardens] prayed that their parish of Sheringham might be secured against them or they be removed unto Edgefield aforesaid.
1 November: William Parke & William Lubbock, being churchwardens of Alby, did complain to me according to the statute that Elizabeth Starling, widow, did within 40 days last past come from Thwaite in this county where she was last before legally settled for 40 days & more as an householder, to settle in a tenement in Alby aforesaid under the yearly value of £10. And that **[f. 21r]** she is likely to be chargeable to the parish of Alby aforesaid.
2º 9bris: Richard Ryall & John Stone have sworn constables of Colby.
Eodem: John Black was the same day sworn in the place of the said

Ryall, being scarce fit scarce fit [sic], & Black the old hired for 134 [sic] & very fit.

3 [November]: a warrant for Elizabeth Thirtle to show me cause for her departure of her service with Richard Ransome, clerk [of Alby], ½ a year yet to come.[204]

7 [November]: a general warrant against Robert Ward & William Ward of Sheringham, seamen, who have threatened Nathaniel Crask [tailor of same], their brother-in-law, to turn him out of his own house.[205]

8 [November]: William Allen & William Wegg sworn constables of Banningham.[206]

3 [November]: a warrant against Elizabeth Thirkle for departing the service of Mr Ransome.

17 [November]: a general warrant against Katherine Greene of Aylsham. She brake up Sam Poole's house & took & converted divers goods of Thomas Weld found there.

19 [November]: a general warrant at large against Giles Sprunt of Skeyton, labourer, & William Starkey of Felmingham, husbandman. Sprunt & Starky had distrained the goods of Susan Davy of Bradfield, whereas they are not named in the warrant of the sheriff & 'tis Starky's [one word illegible] suit. Besides the warrant is mistaken in the day of the county court, November for December.[207]

21 [November]: a warrant of the good behaviour against Thomas Parson of Wickmere, labourer, who is charged to be the reputed father of the male base child whereof Mary Allen was on Saturday last delivered in Ingworth; committed eodem.

[n.d.:] A certificate for discharge of 39 persons & 43 fire hearths for Runton made according to the statute, to which Sir John Palgrave had subscribed. I did subscribe also. And I had so subscribed such another from Beeston, and therein we did declare that a chimney stopped up before the new act was not cha[rgeable].[208]

28 November: a warrant against William Brettingham [yeoman] of Oulton for turning away John Durrant [servant in husbandry] without cause before end of his term.[209]

Eodem: William Park & William Lubbock, churchwardens, & William Langwade one of the overseers of the poor of Alby, did complain unto me that Elizabeth wife of William Heire & one child & a maid did the 13th day of this month come from Hanworth in the said county, where the wife, child & maid had been dwelling for 40 days next before, to settle in a tenement in Alby aforesaid under the yearly value of £10, that is to say 12s. till Michaelmas. And for William Heire they say he was with his father-in-law Chapman the last harvest and that he is a person whose place of settlement is not yet known.

[f. 21v] *[n.d.] 1664:* a warrant against Thomas Warner collector of the fire hearth money money [sic] for wrongful taking distresses of John Pescod & Thomas Marshall.

5⁰ [December]: I heard the case, they being clearly within the first proviso as the parson & churchwardens certified me.

Eodem: Warner had a warrant against John Soame, labourer, for injuring him in the execution of his office.

Eodem: William Callor of Colby, worsted weaver, was by his own confession convicted before me for drawing within 14 days last past near two barrels of beer without licence in Colby aforesaid, for which he saith 12s. is yet owing him. William Barnes & John Herring were present & witnessed near as much.

6 [December]: a general warrant against William Leasy of West Beckham, mason, for enticing away William Brett, whom Sir John Palgrave & myself had ordered to be bound an apprentice unto William Risbrough of Sustead (one officer had only set his seal but two had set their hands to the indenture).

2 [December]: a complaint was duly made to Sir John Palgrave & myself that Mary Lane, being a poor person & likely to be chargeable to the parish of Runton within 40 days came from South Golston[210] to settle in Runton in a tenement under the yearly rent of £10, being a new erected cottage. 12 [December] I signed the warrant.

12 [December]: a warrant against John Fisher to pay Robert Lettle the 10s. remaining of his wages.

Eodem: a warrant to carry coals etc. for Cecily the wife of Robert Pye lately pressed into a ship of the king's, who is not by her work able to keep her 4 children.

Eodem: a warrant to allow a competent relief to William Crow & his wife, being old. Southrepps hath allowed them 6d. whereof they pay 2d. for house rent.

14 [December]: a warrant for Robert Priest & Joseph Ward to be sworn constables of Roughton.

19 [December]: Joseph Ward sworn in place of Thomas Hogan; 23 [December] Robert Priest also sworn.

27 [December]: a complaint by [John] Benington [of Alby] against Samuel Bun [of same] whom for want of sureties for his good behaviour I then sent to the gaol.[211]

Eodem: a new warrant for the good behaviour against William Lacy, as 6 December.

28 [December]: a warrant against Edward Fox [yeoman of Hanworth] for not paying his servant [Richard] Salmon [labourer of Thorpe Market] his wages.[212]

30 [December]: a general warrant against Edmund Bell of Thurgarton who had beat his wife & threatened to kill her & her children.

2 January [1665]: a warrant against Mr James Taylor to pay Robert Ryall his £3 11s. wages or to be brought etc. I heard the case. Mr Taylor paid him 12s. & promised to pay him at our next Lady Day 54s.

Eodem: a warrant for Richard Greene of Northrepps to appear on Monday next, when I intend to take proofs against him for his commonly selling of beer.

[f. 22r] *3 January 1665:* Edmund Clerke the only churchwarden of West Beckham in Norfolk did complain unto me (& so did Christopher Barnwood an inhabitant there) that Sara the wife of Jeffrey Diker of Kettlestone in Norfolk, being great with child, did within forty days last past come from Kettlestone aforesaid to settle in a tenement in West Beckham aforesaid under the yearly value of £10, being a backhouse newly converted into

a cottage, and that she is a person likely to be chargeable to the parish of West Beckham aforesaid. He was housekeeper & now run away ut dicitur.
Eodem: Richard Ellis & Allen Emerson the two churchwardens of Northrepps in Norfolk did complain unto Sir Thomas Rant kt. & myself that John Archer, his wife & child being poor persons & likely to be chargeable to the parish of Northrepps did within 40 days last past come from Gimingham in Norfolk where they were last settled for 40 days & more, & he as householder, to settle in a tenement in Northrepps aforesaid under the yearly value of £10, being a cottage of her father with whom they now cohabit.
13 [January]: a general warrant against John Mason, the runaway apprentice of Robert Ferryer of Paston, blacksmith. He beat his master also.[213]
18 January: I sent Mathew Cooper, the runaway apprentice of John Harris [blacksmith] of Erpingham, to Aylsham bridewell for a month, unless [released] by me or some other.
Eodem: I bound Thomas Pooley [of Aylsham] to his good behaviour praecipue erga Harris. He had been the encourager of Cooper all along, provided him his master at Cringleford & now in coming before me had said Cooper should never [return] to his master Harris his service, do he what he could.[214]
21 [January]: 2 warrants against Peter Abs of Runton & Edmund Clerk of Sheringham for enforcing W. Pull (by colour of my warrant to search for Abs's stolen goods) to enter bond to Clerke for payment of £5 & to confess a judgement to him of £10. Henry Baldwin witness.[215]
Eodem: a general warrant against Robert Swan of Southrepps. He had taken & marked Simpson's sheep.
23 [January]: Richard Bartram & Richard Howard the two churchwardens of the parish of Thorpe Market did complain unto me that Stephen Annis the younger, thatcher, being a poor person & likely to be chargeable to the said parish, did within 40 days last past (that is the 31st day of December last past) come from Northrepps in the said county where he was last before legally settled as a servant or sojourner with Stephen Annis the elder his father, to settle in a tenement in Thorpe Market aforesaid under the yearly value of £10, that is of £3 per annum or thereabouts, with his father-in-law Nicholas Annis & hath married the daughter of [blank].
[f. 22v] *28 January 1665:* [I] sent Robert Coo, Sir John Palgrave's man, to Bridewell for having on two nights run out to dancings, & the first time he was out all night & the last time till midnight, for he would not come home until the dancing was over, though Sir John sent for him. The last time he carried away the key of the hall door to get in again.[216]
Eodem: I signed a licence for Samon of Bradfield to kill meat this Lent, upon the desire of Sir John [Palgrave] for Mrs Gray & her two daughters.[217]
30 [January]: a warrant for Aldborough churchwardens & overseers to distrain Thomas Yaxley for 11s. 2d. & Humphrey Smith for 1s. 3d.
31 [January]: a general warrant against Daniel Banyard of Southrepps, tailor, against whom Thomas Hauser his landlord complain he payeth

no rent. He burns such part of an house as is fallen down, & he threateneth him & his servants who desire to save it & carry it away.
Eodem: a warrant of the good behaviour against Robert Underwood of Gresham, alehousekeeper, charged to be the reputed father to the male bastard child on the body of Mary Barderston of Sustead, spinster.[218]
1 February: a general warrant against Margaret Bell [spinster] of Felmingham who had stolen a goose of Thomas Church [husbandman of same].[219]
4 [February]: a warrant for John Moy, from whom 2 geese were this night stolen & formerly other goods, to search. Richard Watton his son-in-law saith they suspect William Barney. I have required the warrant with[in] 14 days to be returned me with an account of all.
31 January: a general warrant against Richard Allen of Southrepps, cordwainer, for disorders at the widow [Unica] Risbrough's house. The constable sent word but in the end for [sic] forced to come himself.[220]
6 February: the cause was heard & Allen having no sureties for his good behaviour I sent him to the gaol but ordered the constable to let [him] have liberty of 2 days to get sureties. He after was bound.
7 [February]: Allen was bound to his good behaviour & especially towards the widow Risbrough, he in £10 & John Walby [of] Thorpe [Market] & Richard Gilbert [of] Southrepps in £5 apiece.
8 [February]: a warrant for Henry Williams [thatcher of Aylsham] & Thomas Pooley [cooper of same] to prove how they came by a gate & pales (broke or unbroke) they had been seen to carry, and Captain Barker supposeth were his. See 9 [February].
9 [February]: a warrant for Anfillis Lacy of Runton, widow, tomorrow to appear before me, for then I am to take proof against her for keeping an unlicensed alehouse.[221]
Eodem: the like warrant to convict [Elizabeth] Platten of the same, widow.[222]
Eodem: a general warrant against Thomas Copeman for beating his wife.
[f. 23r] *9 February 1665:* I ordered Thomas Pooley & Henry Williams to pay Mr Thomas Barker 5s. (for satisfaction for his gate & two rails) within a month next ensuing & to pay forthwith to the overseers of the poor of Aylsham 6d. apiece etc.[223]
11 February: a warrant to search for coals & fowls stolen from Mrs Dorothy Gryme, the widow of young George Grime of Gimingham. Robert Margetson saith she suspects divers of her servants who live in the towns near about.
10 [February]: The widows Platten & Lacy were both convicted before me for common selling of beer without lawful licence in Runton. And I then granted a warrant to the constables to levy their 20s. apiece thereupon forfeited.[224]
14 [February]: Richard Buttall the only churchwarden & overseer of the poor of the parish of Gunton (the other being removed out of town) did complain unto me (as did Mr Anthony Jermy the minister & William Custance an inhabitant the day before) that William Harmer, his wife & child did within 40 days last past, that is about 3 weeks before, come from Wiveton where they had been last settled (without complaint) & he

as an inhabitant for 40 days & more to settle in a tenement in Gunton aforesaid under the yearly value of £10 by the year (that is of 20s. or thereabout), and that they be poor persons & likely to be chargeable to the said parish of Gunton.[225]
Eodem: a warrant to remove them.
Memorandum: I gave John Browne of Gresham, seaman, a certificate that he had declared to me his purpose to tender himself to Sir Thomas Medow in [Great] Yarmouth for a volunteer in his majesty's fleet. And I required all to let him quietly pass thither, so he were there by Friday next at noon: dated 14 February.
Eodem: William Calk sworn constable of Paston in place of Mr Burroughs.
Eodem: Richard Allen [cordwainer of Southrepps] was [on the] 6th bound by me to his good behaviour, praecipue erga widow Risbrough, & she this day before me released it.[226]
20 [February]: a general warrant against John Boys & John Thirst of Cromer, seaman, who with other had nailed up the doors of John Woolsey's house & after taken of their goods out of the window.
22 [February]: Margaret Barkle, the servant of James Money of Gresham, butcher, was charged to have taken an handkerchief with flour & late in the night with Ellen Berston & Katherine Wilson to have gone to the widow Thoulder's house in Sustead, intending a merry meeting there with some fellows. But the widow would not let it [some pork] be dressed but offered it **[f. 23v]** *22 February 1665, 17 Carolus [II]* back again when they went away, who would not take them, so they were after eaten in the family. She did acknowledge the taking of the flour. Sir John Palgrave & myself sent her to bridewell to be whipped & discharged.[227]
Eodem: We bound Peter Abs of Runton to the good behaviour in @£100 & Edmund Clerke was his surety in £50. We offered to bind Clerke with Abs for surety in the like sums & after to have taken his own security, but he would not, so we sent him to the gaol. They had made use of one & both the warrants I granted, the one against William Pull & his wife & the other to search. Abs was one of the constables but pretended himself sick, so Clerke went to Dawson the other constable, who charged Clerke to assist him, & they arrested Pull & his wife & searched there & found a sack full of wool (which was after acknowledged to be Henry Baldwyn's, who got 30s. composition). But Abs came presently to Pull's and threatened them violently & so went home. Dawson & Clerke carried the prisoners to Abs and all (but Dawson) went into his parlour. There was tampering about an agreement; £30 & after £20 was demanded, and as Abs & Clerke say, £5 & £10 after was offered by Pull but would not do it. So the prisoner[s] were committed to Clerke & Baldwin to keep all night, though they had day room & might have carried them before a justice. They left the prisoners at liberty, and by the importunity of Pull's wife Pull was drawn to give £12, £13 and at last £15. Clerke went to Abs 3 or 4 times to make that bargain.
Pull entered Clerke a bond for £5 [on] 25 December last and acknowledged him a judgement of £10 to be paid at Michaelmas next. And Clerke said he gave his word to Abs but Abs said he had Clerke's bond for payment of the £5 [on] 2 February & the £10 1 November next. And being put to

reconcile the difference, they said Abs had Clerke's word for the £5 & bond for the £10.

Then it was agreed to go to Sir John Palgrave. The prisoners were to stay for Clerke at Gresham alehouse, and Clerke went (with one like a witness) to Chapman's for his daughter, who was to have been chief witness. Chapman tells him his daughter was privily gone away 4 hours before day (having been at Abs's till the night before & then 'tis thought they had advised her going away). The prisoners came on to Sir John Palgrave's & finding him from home returned. Clerke finds out Sir John, who went presently home. There Abs & Clerke complain **[f. 24r]** *1665* against Pull's wife for advising Chapman's daughter to steal yarn[228] from Abs. The party like a witness said she heard Chapman's daughter to say so. Sir John thinking this had been all gave power to all constables in the county by way of addition to my warrant to cause Chapman's daughter to testify. But neither acquainted Sir John with the suspicions they had found nor what Pull & his wife or either of them had said. She had said if extremities were used (which Abs to enforce the composition dreadfully threatened), she & all her friends must be hanged. Clerke had sued Pull for the £5, whereupon he complained. And on the day I heard the case there was a warrant in Abs's hands to press that Pull and other seamen. And he since went away to [Great] Yarmouth & his wife hath absented herself & left her 3 children to the town.

Clerke all along smoothly says he was drawn in by Pull to engage to Abs, but Abs all along talks of the £15 as his money. And the last time (but this) he told me he would take the money from Mr Flint, whom Abs saw laboured for Pull's discharge, though I all along told Abs that Pull should pay him all he owed him & so made it appear, for which I had given Abs day. But Abs at that last time told me he had security & he would give no account of the particulars unless he were required in Chancery. Clerke to draw on Pull had told him that though he then gave those securities to satisfy Abs in his fury, he did not doubt but that Abs would after abate a considerable part. And Abs had said what he would abate it should proceed from himself only.[229]

Eodem: Willis was promised 30s. by Elward & 4 days works & what Willis had of his in his hand, which Willis saith was 2s., Elward 10s. But Elward had not any money & Willis would not trust, so Sir John [Palgrave] undertook [on the] 23rd to end all or return the recognizance to which our hands were set.

10 March: a warrant against the constables of Gresham for having taken Robert Underwood's word & not bringing him before me or any other.

13 [March]: a general warrant against Edmund Everitt [labourer] of Sustead. He is suspected to have stolen much poultry from Mr [Edward] Crosby [of Metton] to whom he tasked etc.[230]

Eodem: a warrant against the said William Elward for cutting & spoiling my wood, granted by Sir John Palgrave. Mr Lock saw him cutting & laying snow on the stub.

14 [March]: 2 general warrants, the one against James Risbrough of Aylsham & the other against Christopher Doughty [butcher] of Tuttington, for taking William Presse [of Alby] his cow **[f. 24v]** *1664/5* [sic] by colour

of a replevin, whereas Presse claimed her for his own & had had her from his father almost 3 years before & 2 years after his father's death. And she was (to be) in part for his board.[231]
Eodem: a general warrant against Abraham Rose [husbandman], a servant of Mr Robert Thexton [clerk], who had put up some 3 pecks of wheat for market more than directed.[232]
Eodem: a general warrant against Jeffrey Fox of Felbrigg, husbandman. He had mixed ling[233] he had digged with 2 loads of ling Thomas Worme had digged. They had 3s. per load, & Fox would engross & dig for 4s. the load.
20 [March]: a general warrant against Robert Burton the father & Robert Burton the son, both of Paston & thatchers. They had stole William Eades's boards & broke down near 20 rods of pales & carried away the pales.[234]
Eodem: William Scottow & John Moore the two overseers of the poor of the parish of Corpusty did complain unto me that William Purdy & Ann his wife did within 40 days last past (within 3 weeks) come from Wood Dalling in this county, where he was last settled for 40 days & more as an apprentice or[235] servant, to settle in a tenement in Corpusty aforesaid under the value of £10 per annum (as an inmate in the cottage of Thomas Cooper, which is let in all but for 10s. the year), and that the said William Purdy & Ann his wife be poor persons & likely to be chargeable to the said parish of Corpusty, and did thereupon pray that the said parish might be of them discharged according to the new act. They had a warrant then under my hand & went to Sir John Palgrave, kt. and bart.
21 [March]: Richard Bennett junior sworn one of the constables of Cromer [in place of] Jo. Miller.
22 [March]: a warrant for making the order in the case of Mary Balderston bastards.[236]
Eodem: a general warrant against Samuel Smith of Metton, labourer, for beating St. Evered.
23 [March]: a warrant to provide maintenance for William Rice, a poor lame man of Suffield, who having married a young wife hath had his 6d. a week formerly allowed him thence taken away.[237]
31 [March]: a general warrant against John Browne of Horning, waterman, for taking a box of linen & woolen of Winifred Graves of Aylsham, which he was to have sent by Jo. Browning to her about Michaelmas last & never sending it.
Eodem: a warrant for Robert Sendall [husbandman of Burgh next Aylsham] to pay Elizabeth Forman [daughter of Susan, the wife of Robert Forman] her ½ year's wages of 9s. & her clothes which he detains, having turned her away.[238]
[f. 25r] *4 April 1665:* a general warrant against Edward Plane of Little Barningham, husbandman, for pulling the left ear of William Claxton, a poor old blind man of their town & throwing a stone at Alice his wife. They said he frequently beat his own wife.
6 April: a warrant against William Crisp, John Allen, Andrew Raven, John Rye, William Bloome, John King, Edmund Watlin & John Collens, poor boys & men of Cromer, for cutting, stealing & spoiling the woods of William Heaslop, the Lady Windham's farmer.

Eodem: a warrant for Winifred Fuller & Elizabeth Ward of Gresham, widows, to deliver the clothes & goods of Rachel Fuller's in their hands unto the said Rachel or the overseers of Cromer, who have allowed her in her sickness of the palsy £3 and upwards. I ordered Richard Bassam to pay her 1s. per week for 20 weeks if she shall so long live, & he to be acquitted of the £3 & use etc.
10 [April]: a warrant to Runton overseers to pay Margaret Worsted's house rent & 12s. 6d. now in arrear or to show cause. She hath been lately sick & her work is so little, but when she was able she did help to relieve her mother.
Eodem: a warrant against Sara Pull, wife of William Pull, for taking away a cow of John Cooke of Runton had in wintering at Mr Ward's, who have since had a calf, which John Cooke was to have & the profit of the cow till Mayday for the firing & house farm of Mary Phillips, widow, her landlady.[239]
Eodem: a general warrant against John Barker of the same, tailor, for beating Cooke's wife & saying he would do justice himself.[240]
14 [April]: a general warrant against John Bishop of Thwaite for using play & common selling drink. Richard Bankes was cheated there of his cloak worth 30s., & the pretence is he sold it for 18d. the pound & took 5s. in part, & that when he found it weighed but about 7 lb., which would come but to 10s. & 6d., he threw back the money & would not proceed.
15 [April]: a warrant of the peace against Edmund Rumbelow of Aylsham, tailor, at & upon the desire & oath of Katherine Greene wife of Edmund Green. He had bid others chop off her neck, who were assaulting her, & said he would do it himself if she came near him, she being a prisoner there.
17 [April]: a warrant of the peace against Katherine Greene upon the oath of Samuel Pooly, who was to have the parlour by agreement & whom she threw stones at, being lame, & brake a spade's helve in breaking ope his doors & after beat Pooley's wife with the broke shaft & threw it at her.
[f. 25v] *17 Aprilis 1665:* William Bacon sworn constable of Thurgarton in the place of Robert Risbrough.
18 [April]: a warrant of the peace against Edmund Rust, husbandman, upon the oath of Ann Thompson of Aylsham, also spinster. He had threatened her, & his wife had thrown a stone at her.
Eodem: a supersedeas of a warrant granted to remove John Reeve & his wife & family or any of them from Aylsham unto Aylmerton as poor persons etc., where he & she have trades & he have in Aylmerton £11. 4s. by the year. He having appealed against the justices' judgement to the next sessions & entered a recognizance there to prosecute his appeal, he had this day told Mr [Oliver] Neave he had £11 4s. per annum, and Mr Neave had him engage it to secure the town. He told him then he should never more be master of it & Mr Neave told him it was not intended he should, so that Mr Neave agree wholly with the pack, Reeve's declared intent being to purchase in Aylsham and the pack's to bind up his Aylmerton estate so as he might not.
19 [April]: a general warrant against Martha Nichols [spinster of Sustead] who had broke the window of William Grice [cordwainer of same].[241]

Eodem: I heard the case, found her very high, chid her & ordered her wood [sic].
Eodem: I signed indentures for Ann Abs, a child of Aylmerton, to serve Ann Tholder of Sustead till 21 or her marriage.
20 [April]: a general warrant at large against James Rivett of Sustead, tailor, who had sold a cow to Audrey, the wife of William Elwood of the same, baker, for £3 9s., whereof she paid him £3 2s. down (and was to deliver her) but he hath since sold her to Dennis Robinson for £3 8s. & hath delivered her to him.[242]
Eodem: a general warrant against Frances Riches of Blickling upon complaint of Richard Smith of the same, malster, who[m] she hath abused by words & saying he had the French pox.
22 [April]: a warrant to apprehend William Cooke of Witton, husbandman, to find sureties of his good behaviour & to be examined concerning the bastardy of his & [sic].[243]
24 [April]: a warrant of the peace granted against Thomas Martins who hath [no] calling or place of residence but the bridewell or gaol, being always of bad behaviour, upon the oath of Margaret his wife, whose goods he first spent & the best clothes off her back, scarce leaving her any clothes, and then separated from her for their horse, as appeareth by his writing under his hand & seal dated 25th of August 1663, drawn by George Bird Esq.
[f. 26r] *24 April 1665:* a general warrant against John Harloe of Southrepps for taking away the goods of Robert Fox of Felmingham in his absence & notwithstanding his own release of the 18th of March last & his agreement Fox should keep in a chamber till Michaelmas.
Eodem: William [Cooke] neither confessing nor denying the bastardy was bound in £10 & 2 £5 [sureties].[244]
25 [April]: Mr Taylor the constable of Aylsham told me that Ra. Greene & Rumbelow are agreed.
26 [April]: John Johnsons sworn constable of Felbrigg in the place of Richard Allen.
28 [April]: a pass for Susan Allen to Walcott. She was born in Holt, she pretendeth she went from Pope there to Walcott to her brother Allen a miller, and inquiring for a service she was taken by Aylmerton watch.
Eodem: a warrant to search for John Donne's lasts etc. & to bring Lawrence Cooke (his apprentice) before me etc. He went to sea & sets up for himself & hath got his master Donne's lasts etc.
29 [April]: a warrant for [blank] to be sworn constable of Sustead.[245]
1º Maii: I took the information & examination against & of Lawrence Cooke & bound John Dun to the next sessions at Norwich to prosecute, and I then sent Lawrence Cooke to the gaol.
Eodem: I sent Bridget Potts, a girl of 16 years & assigned prentice to Thomas Wells of Aldborough, to Bridewell to be there mod[erately?] whipped & forthwith discharged. She had run away 6 times from him since Christmas last & without any cause but her roguing disposition.
2 [May]: John Drewry sworn constable of Thurgarton in the place of John Bacon.
Eodem: a warrant against the widow Ward & Margaret Miller (the wife of

William Miller, who liveth from her) for to pay the watchmen [who] yesternight watched at Sheringham in their course.[246]

3 [May]: The widow Ward gave satisfaction but Margaret Miller would not, was brought before me, had no sureties for her appearance at sessions & good behaviour, so [was] committed.[247]

7 [May]: Thomas Rust was apprehended yesternight & now brought before me for that Anthony Greene (they being both of Aylsham) did about[248] 11 & 12 o'clock at night see the said Rust carrying homewards a great burden of furze. And suspecting he had stole them & endeavouring to discover who he was and he not willing to discover himself, thereupon Greene laid hold of Rust's furze & Rust threw them down and with his fur[ze] hook struck Greene upon both his hands & after said, What harm have I done. Whereupon Greene said, You have wounded me, and I will not put it up, and then went to the watchmen, who apprehended Rust & thence to Mr Taylor, who looked to the wounds. Rust saith he told him at first his name but Greene saith he told it him not, neither knew he who he was till discovered by a candle from a neighbour's house there. **[f. 26v]** *1665* Thomas Callow of Blickling, sworn, saith for Rust that Rust was his fur[ze] maker & had made up the burden to carry home at night & that the same was carried by his cart to Jo. Some's house at the Dog, where he carried the load, and that Rust took thence the furze to carry to his house. I agreed them that Rust should pay Greene within 3 weeks 2s. 6d. & the charge of his cure.

7° Maii: a warrant against old John Tuck [labourer of Aylsham] for breaking a gate & carrying away part thereof of the said [Anthony] Greene [grocer of Aylsham].[249]

10 [May]: a general warrant against John Thoulder [cordwainer of Sustead] who stole a yard & half of green blanket off of the bed of Ann Pye [spinster of Gresham] this morning while she slept thereon. She saw him going out at her door.[250]

Eodem: William Ransome sworn constable of Sustead in William Risbrough's stead.[251]

Eodem: a warrant of the peace against Stephen Empson of Blickling, husbandman, upon the oath of Ann the wife of James Bennett [cordwainer] of the same. He spurned her & threatened to lame her, & it was for her passing in their usual way to her house (she hireth of him) & he would lay [sic] inconveniently etc.[252]

Eodem: a warrant of the good behaviour against Goodman Nicholas Coe [labourer] of Norwood Barningham, who is charged by Ellen Richardson [spinster of Runton] to have got her with child. For want of sureties I sent him to the gaol 11 May.[253]

12 [May]: a general warrant against William Roberts of North Walsham, miller. He had sold an iron for a crow[-bar] to Annyson of Swafield for 12d. & taken a penny & 2 jugs of beer & was to have the rest when the work was done for which the same was bought. Annison put an handle or staff on to the iron & wrought with it, and Roberts, [who] before the work [was] done took all away, denieth it. Annyson's wife complain of the injury & Roberts threaten suit.

Eodem: a warrant of good abearing against the widow Coates, the

alehousekeeper in Fringe, for buying or taking to pawn in her alehouse the blanket in 10 May for 18d. & refusing to restore it [to] Ann Pye till satisfied.[254]
15 [May]: Christopher Freeman was sworn constable of Blickling in the stead of William Turner, who is removed to Aylsham.
Eodem: Stephen Empson bound to the peace, Mr Daniel Wiseman & [blank] Aldrich sureties.
Eodem: a warrant of the good behaviour against James Cooke of Witton, who 3 times brake open the door & 3 times rescued William Cooke abovesaid his brother, then in custody upon my warrant of 22 April. His mother promised satisfaction & this day when it was demanded threatened suit & gave base language.
17 [May]: a warrant for relief of Mary Downing & her four children, her husband being this day carried to the gaol (or show cause).
[f. 27r] *17 Maii 1665:* a warrant to the surveyors of Thwaite highways.
22 [May]: a general warrant against Thomas Carr, labourer, for wounding Ja. Risbrough's prentice. Aylsham.
Eodem: another against Edmund [Twine?] & John Richardson, labourers, [of] Runton for taking away furze off of Aylmerton common digged by Hillon Bessesson.
Eodem: another against Thomas Pratt of Paston for taking away cravises[255] out of the ped[256] of Thomas Revett of Cromer, pedder.
23 [May]: a general warrant against Edmund Cubitt & Robert Slap [husbandmen], the two surveyors of Trimingham, who in their way day with their company threw down a dike of Mr Clerke's [of Sidestrand yeoman].[257]
Eodem: a warrant to send John Richardson of Runton to bridewell. He confesseth the taking up of ling left by a cart in Aylmerton, & Dawson & Bessesson said they were as much as 4 fur[ze] faggots.[258]
Eodem: a notice to Henry Webster to appear before me for ending the difference about his taking a distress for Henry Baldwin's chimney money.
24 [May]: a warrant to Blickling officers to relieve Elizabeth Bun, who hath 4 small children & hath sold her bed & bedstead. And he [her husband] owe more than he is worth & hath from a week before Christmas been imprisoned by Sir John Hobart for £20. He hath offered a pightle [that] cost £18 for £15 thereof & 'tis refused, his father-in-law to engage for the rest.
25 [May]: a warrant of the peace against Ann Burrell & Mary Yarne of Aylsham, spinsters, who beat & threatened to be the death of Elizabeth, the wife of John Annison [labourer] of the same, because she had related that the widow Yarne their mother had invited her to the Black Boys to lie with a gentleman (who came down in his coach to get Sir John Potts arrested).[259]
29 [May]: Ann Burrell & Mary Yarne bound & so was Elizabeth Annison upon my cousin [Francis] Corye's warrant, which was older than mine, but they forthwith agreed, & I caused Annison to have[260] her 2s. 6d. back again.[261]
Eodem: a warrant in order to the good behaviour against Stephen Fisher of Aylsham, labourer, for bidding Mr Taylor the constable a turd in his

teeth & refusing twice to watch, once in the Winchester watch in his course & the other time at Aylsham fair last.[262]

Eodem: Thomas Tolling & Christopher Money[263] the two overseers of the poor of the parish of Suffield, & William Fisher one of the churchwardens there, and Mr [Pocke?] the chief constable, did complain unto me that Robert Fox, carpenter, is a person likely to be chargeable to the said parish, and that he within 40 days last past (that is about 3 weeks since) came to settle with his mother in a tenement in Suffield aforesaid under the yearly value of **[f. 27v]** *1665* £10 (vidzt. of 20s.) from Felmingham in this county, where he was (with his wife & 3 children) last before for 40 days & more settled as an householder. And [they] craved that Suffield might be of him discharged according to the statute.

Eodem: I signed a warrant for Fox his removing unless etc.

30 [May]: a general warrant against William Ixworth, Thomas Cocke & Christian Tuck. They were tippling at her house all Sunday at night last, & on Monday Ixworth's wife sent Henry Sprunt their boy for him to come home, & she threatened him, & his master after accordingly beat him & brake his head & made 20 black & blue spots with his cudgel.

31 [May]:[264] a warrant to bring Pooley & Williams before me to answer the not performing my order made 9 February 1665 & to be proceeded with.

Eodem: a warrant to Aylsham surveyors against defaulters.

1⁰ Junii: Mary Can sware that Stephen Fisher on Saturday beat her with his fist on her cheek & drew blood. See 29 [May]. I sent Fisher to the gaol for want of sureties.

Eodem: Robert Jackson the only churchwarden & Richard Robins & [blank] overseers of the poor of the parish of Itteringham & James Empson constable there did complain to me that Alice Bennett,[265] a poor base child, is likely to be chargeable to the parish & that it (being about 6 years of age) came from Buxton etc., where it was born & ever since hath dwelt, within forty days last past (that is, within a month last past) to settle with her mother & father-in-law (being also poor persons) in a tenement in Itteringham aforesaid under the yearly value of £10 (vidzt. 25s. per annum) & prayed that the said parish might be of the said Alice secured or discharged according to the new act.

Eodem: they had my warrant.

2 [June]: a general warrant against Henry Some of Aylsham, fishmonger, a surveyor, who hath threatened Thomas Empson (6 times & bound it by oath, God damn him) that he would cut him in pieces whensoever he met him. He also said that the Empsons were bastards. Empson had formerly sent an able man into the ways, and upon Some's dislike of him Empson came this day in himself & in the noon while or when he was going in again these words, threats & oaths were used.

5 [June]: a general warrant against Robert Underwood by Elizabeth his wife, whom he had this evening beaten & spurned & thrown down a pair of stairs.

6 [June]: Frances Reynolds [spinster] of Bodham charged John Thomason [labourer], alias John Shropshire because he came with Mr Franckland thence, **[f. 28r]** *1665* to be the father of the bastard she's now quick with.

Eodem: a warrant for his apprehension etc.[266]
Eodem: a general warrant against Henry Soame, fishmonger, for detaining George Grout his brickman's wages & throwing a brick back into the house he was in because he would not work without wages.
9th [June]: a general warrant against Robert Branding of Swanton Abbot [worsted weaver]. He had arrested Thomas Treat of Westwick [husbandman]. Branding's wife had put her husband's name as a bailiff into the bottom of the warrant.[267]
Eodem: Samuel Beales & Thomas Smith the two churchwardens of the parish of Runton did complain unto me that Nicholas Coe did within 40 days last past come from Norwood Barningham in the said county where he was last before legally settled for 40 days next before to settle in a messuage (with one John Breese) in Runton aforesaid under the yearly value of £10 (that is of 40s.), and that the said Coe hath since married a wife, and that he & she be both like to be chargeable to the said parish of Runton, and crave that their parish might be secured or discharged according to the provision of the late act of parliament. They say they have no free houses but their poor are crowded on heaps.[268]
Eodem: I signed a warrant for their remove.
Eodem: a warrant general against Henry Ampleford of Holt, gentleman. He had long had a pick[269] with Thomas Dall his man (& that likely for his mistress's sake), & as he had often threatened him, yesterday so soon as he had helped him up on horse, he with a cudgel brake his, his said man Dall's, pate. And as he saith there had then been no word or cause of discontent (but his mistress was then abroad).
Eodem: a warrant against Thomas Rising of Felmingham, butcher, for threatening to take Elizabeth Rising his sister out of the service of John Hickes [butcher of same], all her year save 10 days being yet to be served out. He formerly had taken her out of another's service & kept her till she had slit her clothes & then her own sister clothed her & put her out to this Hickes. The girl is 16 & will not go to him, & Hicks thinks it's to disappoint him & place her with a neighbour.[270]
10 Junii: a warrant of the good behaviour against the abovesaid Robert Branding [worsted weaver of Swanton Abbot] who, besides his first offence, when John Springall the **[f. 28v]** *1665* constable [of Swanton Abbot] served him this[271] morning with my warrant did desire to hear the same read, & the constable parting with it for[272] Branding's wife to read, it was kept from him. And the said Branding said that it might light a tobacco pipe. And when the constable with the complainant & his witnesses came hither, Richard Beare brought the same to the constable and now tells me Branding shall appear before me on Monday next.[273]
11 [June]: a warrant to search for a calf running with the cow in Metton stolen since last Friday from John Bond of Roughton (not [paid?]).[274]
12 [June]: Richard Paull & John Johnson the two overseers of the poor of the parish of Felbrigg did complain unto me that Dadlesse, [widow?] & a blind old woman, came within 40 days (that is about a week since) from Town Barningham where she last before lived & was settled as a sojourner for 40 days & more to settle in a tenement in Felbrigg (with Edmund Bell her son-in-law as a sojourner) under the yearly value of

£10, that is of about £4 per annum.

Eodem: a warrant at large against Edmund Everett of Metton [labourer] for stealing [John] Bond's calf. He was accused by Elizabeth Dixon [spinster, wife of William Dixon, lathriver of Sustead] to whom he brought veal.[275]

Eodem: an indented order for Henry Barwick [yeoman of Sheringham] & Henry Webster [revenue collector of same].[276]

Eodem: Robert Branding of Swanton Abbot in the county of Norfolk, worsted weaver, [bound] in £10, Richard Beare & Joseph Beare of the same, worsted weavers, [bound] in £5 apiece, conditioned that the said Robert Branding shall appear at the next quarter sessions of the peace to be held in at [sic] the shire house at the Castle of Norwich & for his good behaviour in the meantime.[277]

13 [June]: a general warrant against John Hanes, linen weaver, Richard Pycroft, worsted weaver, John Sprunt, worsted weaver, William Sprunt, husbandman, Edmund Wilkins, husbandman, & John Snelling, thatcher, & all of Swanton Abbot, for setting made furze of Samuel Hynes [labourer of same] on fire, which burnt many standing furze also & might have hazarded the town. It was on the king's birthday when they were drunk, & had not help come the fire had run further.[278]

Eodem: a warrant against William Austen [yeoman of Paston] for putting John Reeve without cause out of his service & not paying him his wages.[279]

[f. 29r] *14 Junii 1665:* a warrant of the peace against Humphrey Ward of Worstead, grocer, who upon a wager laid with Abraham Moll & near won, fell upon the said Moll & beat & bruised him etc.

Eodem: a warrant with Sir John Palgrave to order Runton officers to pay Elizabeth (the wife of Launcelot Richardson, who half a year before was pressed into the king's sea-service) 5s. for her present want, she lying now in, and further to maintain her & her two children what she cannot earn to make a livelihood by her work.

15 [June]: a general warrant against Robert Marfield of Felmingham, worsted weaver. He was heard by Thomas Starky [of same] to have said on the king's birthday, when Mr Needs prayed for the king in his prayers before his sermon, that upon his head[280] his crown might long flourish, that that should not be long. I bound him to the sessions, who discharged him.[281]

Eodem: I took the informations against & examination of Cicely Abbes, wife of Thomas Abbes of Aylmerton, weaver, for stealing a pinner[282] her husband sold a woman at the common staithe for 18d. (& a child's shirts which was lost) & divers other linen, which were by him returned. I sent her then to the gaol. I hear she was branded.

Eodem: a general warrant against William Crow & his wife of Southrepps. She had borrowed 12d. of Ellen Watson [spinster of same], & when she came after the day of payment to demand it, she told her she would pay her with her husband's weeding hook & asked where she met her, & she alleges he also gave foul words to Richard Dix, lathriver, who came with Ellen Watson, she being his sister-in-law.[283]

18 [June]: a warrant to provide an house for Nicholas Coe [of Norwood Barningham], his wife being fallen sick by her lying in [the minister] Mr

Lock's barn. I had made one before.[284]
19 [June]: a warrant according to law to whip Ann Eastwick a wandering beggar taken at Wickmere & then to pass her to Itteringham, where as she say she was born.[285]
Eodem: a general warrant against John Bishop of Aylsham for not watching because Mr Taylor would not go to the cross to give him his charge.
Eodem: a general warrant against John Buttivant, tailor, & Richard Prunyett, husbandman, of Colby for beating William Barnie [tailor of same] his wife.[286]
Eodem: I signed Sheringham poor rate we then perfected; Gregory Christmas then licensed.
[f. 29v] *21 Junii 1665:* a general warrant against John Allen, oatmealmaker, for taking goods from William Barne (both of Colby) his old wife had turned over to him but still kept the possession of when Barne was gone with his whore.
26 [June]: a general warrant against Nathaniel Woodrow, cooper, for his taking a sheep of Mathew Panck, oatmealmaker & both of Cromer.[287]
Eodem: a warrant for William Austen [yeoman] to receive John Reive or pay him 15s. or otherwise to appear etc. (Paston).[288]
Eodem: a general warrant against [blank] Rix, an apprentice, for running away from Robert Hall his master. Aylsham.
28 [June]: at [an] old complaint of [Robert] Marfield & information that Reyner & his [Thomas Starky's] son William Starky could say somewhat material against Marfield, I granted my warrant for them to come before me, to inform what they severally knew thereabout.[289]
29 [June]: a warrant against John Callin of Aldborough, worsted weaver, for beating & bruising William Child, one of the wardsmen, for giving him notice as he was commanded by Mr Wittaker, one of the constables, that his course with others was to watch in the Winchester watch this night. He was to bring sureties.
30 [June]: a warrant of the good behaviour against John Money of Sustead, butcher. He keeps company with Margaret, wife of Thomas Martins, & is now gone away with her and would have his wife sell her cows to trade with as a butcher. But his wife fears 'tis but to maintain the trade with his whore, Martins's wife.
1 Julii: Miles Skerrett sworn one of the constables of Gimingham.
Eodem: a warrant for Robert Wilson of Cromer, blacksmith, forthwith to inform me who it was he heard say that in 24 hours he could raise an hundred horse, or in case he deny it [a warrant for] Edward Jex of Northrepps, brick burner, who said in Nicholas Smith's & others' hearing that he heard Robert Wilson say he heard one say so or to such purpose. It is supposed to be Dennis Bonner.
3 [July]: a general warrant against George Brook by [blank] Pierson. 5 [July] I agreed them.[290]
5 [July]: a general warrant against [blank] Paule of Felbrigg for taking away a skep of bees. They were a flight lighted in Morris his yard & by him hivered. Morris hath no bees & Pawle great store.
Eodem: I sent John Thoulder to Aylsham Bridewell for a month. His

mother first desired his apprehension & before me his acquittal & after that he might there be held to work.

[f. 30r] *7 Julii 1665:* a warrant against Thomas [Grey] & Thomas Fitt, both of Bessingham, labourers, for refusing to assist William Greve, a constable of Sustead, to convey John Thoulder (last mentioned) to Bridewell, though he required & I also commanded them, so as the constable was forced to bring him home & carry him the next day. They were in Sustead at his alehouse when he first charged them to assist in bringing Thoulder before me, so as he could have no other to the Bridewell.[291]

Eodem: a general warrant against Orpha Walby of Thorpe [Market, spinster] for reporting that James Amis of the same was (the last Sunday sevennight) naught[292] with her, the widow Samon & smithy Paul's daughter Ann.[293]

Eodem: a warrant in which Sir John Palgrave was to join to order Cawston churchwardens & overseers to cure Mary Jary her scald head & otherwise to relieve her according to her wants, she lying on a lock of straw almost starved as the widow Hunt complained.

Eodem: liberty given Priscilla Argent to procure her a service by the next petty sessions or to be there to be retained. If her [name] had not been mistaken both [sic] had been sent to bridewell for living out of service.[294]

13 [July]: a general warrant against John Oakely of North Walsham, labourer, for beating Thomas Mautby & his wife, being drunk & swearing.

14 [July]: Edward Clerke sworn constable of Sidestrand.

Eodem: James Jempson of Itteringham, glover, retained Priscilla Argent for a year to begin at Michaelmas next for 30s. wages & 4d. paid her in hand, & her mother promised by that time she should have convenient clothes provided her to fit her for service. And all this was transacted before me.[295]

Eodem: 2 warrants, the one to Aylmerton constables to inform themselves of the widow Reeve's 7 sons, daughters & grandchildren late come thither from [Great] Yarmouth & to certify me. One is said to be sick. The other [warrant] to Cromer [constables] against such as go & come frequently without necessary occasions to [Great] Yarmouth & as are come thence to dwell at Cromer & as are thought to bring dead persons' clothes or stuff thither (to the infecting all) from [Great] Yarmouth to Cromer.[296]

[f. 30v] *17 Julii 1665:* a warrant for Southrepps churchwardens & overseers to pay 3s. to the widow Purgall for her 4 weeks keeping a poor child, or to show cause.

21 [July]: a warrant for Sheringham constables to require the man that came with Beatrice Tracy & Susan Rissick from [Great] Yarmouth. The man is said to have come out of the pest house & to have all his family dead of the plague; Beatrice [is said] to have been a keeper of the persons sick of the plague & now to have a plague sore. They brought two horse loads of stuff said to be the the [sic] stuff & clothes of persons dead of the plague & Sara Tracy in whose house they now be got [is] to keep privately in the same & to bury the infected goods and to set a guard upon them to keep them in.[297]

Eodem: a warrant to require [John] Tod, wife & 3 children to go back to

Edgefield according to law & our & the sessions' orders within 24 hours after notice or else to be removed thither. Sir John [Palgrave]'s hand was to be also had.[298]
22 [July]: Sir John Palgrave & myself granted a warrant against Mr Edward Lomb [gentleman of Cawston], the chief constable, to appear on Monday following by one of clock at Norwood Barningham hall, that we might there examine & take proof of his[299] misdemeanours we were that day acquainted with by the complaints of Mary & Priscilla Argent [of Cawston]. We met, took examinations, & referred it to our sessions.[300]
26 [July]: a warrant to Ingworth churchwardens & overseers to provide an habitation for John Woods, his wife & child of 7 weeks old. They are now lying in the church porch.
Memorandum: the 28th [of July] Ingworth overseers were with me and say Mr [Oliver] Neave bade them let him lie in the church porch.
27 Julii: I kept the sessions at Fakenham. We had nine justices there.
29 [July]: Christopher Reynolds & James Smith both of Blickling did take oath that Margery[301] Smith widow. [sic] Christopher Freman constable there saith that he saw two half barrels laid in by the brewer & that he forbade her upon Tuesday to sell the same out, and that she said she would and another said said [sic] she should draw in spite of them. I then granted my warrant to levy 20s. of her goods etc.
Eodem: a warrant of the peace against Robert Stanton of North Walsham [labourer]. He had struck William Roberts [labourer of same] 2 blows with a whin scythe & cut him on his left arm & head.[302]
31 [July]: Robert Stanton was bound to the peace. He say he was assaulted causelessly by [William] Roberts & that he cut his own arm with his own whin scythe & acknowledgeth that as last [sic], with a thrust of his own, he brake Roberts's head.[303]
[f. 31r] *1º August 1665:* a general warrant against Mathew Leverington. He hath taken away a kettle of Margaret Dunthorne (who is a washer) where it was set for swill, supposing it a kettle of Mary Smith (who sold hers to Mrs Greene) & who owed rent to Mr Leverinton or his mortgagee.
3 [August]: a warrant for [blank] of Beeston to answer the not employing his apprentice.[304]
2 [August]: a warrant against 3 pease stealers of Cromer to appear on Friday pomer[idiano?].[305]
Eodem: a general warrant against John Hall[306] a shirman or dyer who keepeth a shop at North Walsham. He took a piece of tartin of Francis Ducker [labourer of Hanworth] to dye and first excused the not returning it & since denies it.[307]
4 [August]: the 3 pease stealers were before me. One confessed a handful, the other[s] each ½ a peck apiece. Elizabeth Swan offered for satisfaction a day's work in harvest & Mary Beare to make full satisfaction for her handful & Susan Dickthorne the 3rd being a poor silly lame wench he forgave.
Eodem: a warrant for John Welden to [sic — who?] live in the town house with women with whom he is suspected to be incontinent being about 21 & fit for service, forthwith to provide himself a service & abiding elsewhere as he would avoid Bridewell, where he will find both.

Eodem: Michael Wilson's wife saith that her husband did take John Williams for his apprentice and that to keep him they have undone themselves. She hath set him to keep cows (when any would have him) and at other times to spin, where he will earn scarce anything. The agreement is set in the warrant. See 3⁰ [August].[308]

7 [August]: a warrant against Nicholas Balding for departing or putting up his clothes to depart the service of William Cooke of Sheringham, more than ½ his year being yet to serve.

8 [August]: a general warrant against Nicholas Smith the bailiff & William Thaxter of Sustead. They have taken £5 worth of Samuel Bunn's goods & left them with G. Brooke & he know not why, but they say they will answer their taking.

12 [August]: a general warrant against Ann the wife of Benjamin Granger of Blickling. She beat James Grand's wife [Elizabeth of same] for asking money of another woman she owed to James Grand.[309]

Eodem: I having had my men's chamber robbed, where I lost 2 sheets, one off of each bed, & my boy a shirt & his best breeches, had in suspicion Margaret Coxfer. The person had on a red waistcoat & black hood or hat, but I rather suspect Mary Turner & Elizabeth Smith, for they the day before had **[f. 31v]** knocked off the hinges off of my door at Metton, & much of my ceiling there is broke a pieces & carried away. I hear that part is in Webster's house. They might come to make their peace & finding every one out of the way might make [off with] the booty.

12 [August]: a warrant of the peace against William Bower of Wickmere, tailor, upon oath of Robert Sparrow of the same [cordwainer]. He threatens to kill his wife & child & maim him. He say that Sparrow would with a pitchfork have run it in his guts, & Sparrow threatened to strike him down with a pole.[310]

13 [August]: John Powle & Thomas Abs the two churchwardens of the parish of Aylmerton did complain unto me that John Laurence, Ann his wife & their child, being a daughter Jean, with which the said Ann was then great, and John Smith, Jean Smith & Sara Smith did within 40 days last past come from Great Yarmouth in this county where they were last before legally settled, Laurence as an householder & the Smiths as natives, to settle in Aylmerton aforesaid in a tenement or cottage newly converted under the yearly value of £10 (vizdt. of about £2) with the widow Reive, and that they be all poor persons and likely to be chargeable to the said parish of Aylmerton, and prayed that their said parish might be of them discharged or otherwise secured according to the late statute. Memorandum: they came thither only to avoid the danger of the plague in [Great] Yarmouth, therefore no warrant was presently granted for their remove back.

13⁰ [August]: I gave day to Calthorpe officers to inform if they found that Margaret Coxfer was anywhere settled for 40 days after she was settled with them for 49 days (whereupon Sir John Palgrave & myself with Sir Thomas Rant's approbation had 10 August predicto settled her), & in the meantime I ordered Baxter with who[m] she had lived these 49 days to let her stay with him for her money, & the officers to agree them if there were any difference for the place or price.[311]

Eodem: a warrant for Edward Mony & Henry Crow to be sworn constables of Bessingham, their houses being furthest off.[312]
Eodem: Edward Money sworn constable, and a new warrant against Robert Ewayn, who is one of the 2 next & can write & read, Crow being unsufficient.
16 [August]: John Spurrell sworn constable of Metton.
21 [August]: a warrant against young [Thomas] Webster [woolcomber of Metton]. He is supposed to have stolen a fighting cock of Thomas Colby's [tailor of Alby].[313]
[f. 32r] *25 August 1665:* a warrant of the peace against Thomas Starky of Felmingham upon the oath of Eleanor Starky his daughter-in-law, whom he yesternight would have struck but missed her & threatened her to be the death of her & bound it with the oath of By God & as she saith he had often laid in a dike's holl. She saith he & his son (being a boy) do little but live by their wits.[314]
Eodem: a warrant against Thomas Buck of Felbrigg, labourer. Complaint of Nicholas Steward.
26 [August]: he was brought before me & confessed the taking of as much barley of Mr Windham's off of the swath as contained a sheaf, and I in pity to his wife & children sent him to bridewell to be whipped & so forthwith to be discharged.
Eodem: a general warrant against Mary Tylbury widow [of Southrepps], who went up a ladder & stole about ½ a bushel of wheat from William Bowen, carpenter [of same]. Elizabeth Crow his maid saw her go up & take it.[315]
28 [August]: a general warrant against George Hansell of Hevingham for not paying Mat. Armes, his journeyman tailor, who wrought with him 3 weeks lacking one day & was then turned off. He demanded 2s. per week & Hansell offered 22d. Armes demanded 2s. or otherwise his wages at the week's end but Handsell continued him for 20 days & gave him only 16d.
29 [August]: a warrant against Southrepps churchwardens & overseers for not paying to the widow her [blank] her 15d. per week for [blank] weeks etc.
30 [August]: a warrant for the churchwardens & overseers of Calthorpe to approve of Margaret Coxfer's dwelling with Thomas Lubbock till Michaelmas, unless they can provide better for her elsewhere.[316]
31 [August]: Laurence Monyman & Thomas Slop the two churchwardens of the parish of Knapton did make complaint unto me that Richard Mittick, worsted weaver, & his wife did within 40 days (that is about 3 weeks) last past come from the parish of St. Margaret in the city of Norwich, where he was last before legally settled for 40 days & more as an householder, to settle in a tenement (with his mother) in Knapton aforesaid under the yearly value of £10 (that is, of 14s. or thereabout). And that he the said Richard[317] & his wife then were & yet are poor persons & likely to be chargeable to the said parish of Knapton. They hear that all three have but one bed amongst them & the house have not room for another.
Eodem: They had a warrant.[318]
[f. 32v] *3 7bris 1665:* a general warrant against Robert Moyses [labourer

of Alby] (William Langwad's man) for beating Peter Haw [husbandman of Hanworth] (Stephen Starling's) man without any cause given.
Eodem: I bound him [Robert Moyses] in £10 & William Moyses of Erpingham husbandman, his brother & Hob's man (who is worth more than £20), in £10 for Robert's peace.[319]
Eodem: a general warrant against Edmund Bell of Thurgarton, labourer, for threatening to kill his wife & her children or some of them & making them lie abroad.
4 [September]: he appeared, justified himself & threatened she should suffer worse, whereupon I sent him to Bridewell.
5 [September]: a warrant for Mr Webster. He came, & I ordered Richard Duffield to pay Webster 6s. & to have his mare again, for Duffield had tendered offered [sic] 2s., but it was not for the kitchen fire hearth but for all. There would otherwise [be] but 5s. due. But Duffield was in danger by having charged Webster with felony & charged Sustead constables with him.
Eodem: a general warrant against Gilbert Parker of North Walsham, husbandman. He had threatened with his knife drawn to stab to the heart Mr Robert Blofield coming for the lecture at North Walsham for a largesse and threatened to meet with him another day or elsewhere.
11 [September]: a general warrant against Thomas Angell of Runton. His sister threw water of Ann [sic] coming home as an harvest lady, & she bad her throw her bastard, from which occasion Thomas Angell called her whore & said she had murdered her bastard & buried it in Plumstead churchyard. (She was Mr Wilson's servant)
[n.d.]: a warrant with Sir Thomas Rant for shutting up Austin of Paston, it being thought his 2 children, wife & servant are all dead of the plague. The servant is said to have fetched somewhat from Bacton.
25 [September]: a warrant against Austin Parker for not paying £3 4s. for part of [blank].
Eodem: a warrant against Thomas Otty [labourer of West Beckham] for taking in, & after the sending away privily taking in again, Katherine Thurstan [a poor person], who is since delivered of a bastard in West Beckham.[320]
Eodem: a warrant against Peter Margetson [husbandman] of Gunton for turning away Dorothy Parker & not paying her her wages. Paid 2s. 8d., rem[ainder] 14s. 4d.[321]
26 or 7 [September]: a warrant against the grandfather [Thomas Thurstan of Billingford] to discover the fraud in bringing Katherine Thurstan privily into West Beckham, where the Saturday before she was delivered of a base man child.[322]
29 [September]: a warrant against Thomas Eastick [thatcher of Elsing] returnable to myself to examine & bind over, he being charged to be its reputed father. Mr Oliver Neave I hear bound him.
[f. 33r] *2 8bris 1665:* Robert Learner, one of the churchwardens, & James Tower & William Duffield the two overseers of the poor of the parish of West Beckham complained to me that Katherine Thurstan now or late of the parish of St. Giles in the city of Norwich, spinster, did within forty days last past come to settle in a tenement in West Beckham aforesaid

under the yearly value of £10[323] & that she was last before legally settled in the said parish of St. Giles as a servant (with one Thomas Long without St. Giles's gates), and that since such her coming to settle in West Beckham as aforesaid she hath been there delivered of a male bastard child, and that she & her said child be poor persons & likely to be chargeable to the said parish of West Beckham, and thereupon craved that the said parish of West Beckham might be of them and either of them severally discharged. She lived 5 months at St. Giles, 14 days at Elsing with Eastick, 14 days with her father at Billingford, 3 weeks at West Beckham & thence she went to Felbrigg & after 14 days' absence returned to West Beckham & in 14 days after was delivered of her bastard, which was on Saturday morning last was a sevennight.
Eodem: a general warrant against William Well [fisherman] & William Shepheard [seaman] of Sheringham, the first for taking in & concealing a [Great] Yarmouth person, the other for abusing Thomas Webb the constable [and seaman of Sheringham].[324]
3º [October]: upon proof that Shepheard had said to Webb, who reproved him for calling Tobias Butcher, Whoring rogue, cheating rogue, peevish rogue & thievish rogue, & saying he would prove him so, by saying, Fie for shame you thus to abuse him, no flesh can endure it. Shepheard thereupon said to Webb, You great headed rogue, you had best take his part, & Webb replying, I am as God made, and he [who] made my head made your snotty nose. Shepheard further said, Then you are Mr Constable, I wonder what rogues made you a constable. I could shit a better constable, the devil take you, you will be meddling. Shepheard also after the first broil said to Webb, You Goodman Jackanapes, what will you do to me Goodman Constable, Goodman Turd, etc.
Eodem: Confessed by [William] Well that he had taken in Susan Harman from [Great] Yarmouth to the endangering Sheringham with the sickness. Upon the townsmen's offence [he] sent her away yet after privily took her in, first denied her with imprecations yet near the month's end defended the taking her so in, saying he would keep her spite of their teeth. Both [men bound] to good behaviour.[325]
[f. 33v] *5 October 1665:* Samuel Beales & Thomas Smith the two churchwardens of Runton made complaint unto me that Thomas Proudfoote & his wife came within 40 days last past from Beeston Regis in this county where he & she were last before legally settled (as sojourner with[326] [blank] Proudfoote his father) to settle in a tenement in Runton aforesaid under the yearly value of £10 (being a new constructed cottage contrary to the statute of 31 Elizabeth) and that he & she be poor persons and likely to be chargeable to the parish of Runton aforesaid. Given a warrant upon it.
13 October: a warrant for Thomas Wells to place Margaret Coxfer alias Cockman with him, who by order of the sessions 3 October [was] sent to & placed in Aldborough, till the inhabitants should show good cause to the contrary to this court.
15 [October]: a general warrant against Thomas Copeman [labourer of Thurgarton] for [stealing] Ann Pye's kettle & wooden dish.[327]
16 [October]: I heard the case.

Eodem: I signed Sir Thomas Rant's warrant for removing William Harmer & his wife to Gunton.[328]
Eodem: a warrant against Margetson of Gunton to pay [blank] Parker 2s. brass & 1s. arrears.[329]
17 [October]: a warrant to Runton officers to relieve Elizabeth Breese who hath the falling sickness & Elizabeth Richardson who hath 2 children & her husband pressed away. Or show cause.
20 [October]: a warrant of the peace against James Risbrough of Aylsham, tailor, upon the oath of Francis Balls, whose head he brake, whose gloves he took up and conveyed away, & whom he threatened to take such course with [that] he should never go more upon green grass (if he met him again, as he had drawn blood).
Eodem: a warrant to pay Thomas Thurkle his 12d. per week & arrear. Poor & diseased.
Eodem: a general warrant against Margaret Tyler. She heretofore pretended Francis Cully her landlord's son had got her with child, & now again saith he hath got the child she is now with. She came part of the way & then would come no further but said she would drown herself. Cully denies all.
Eodem: a general warrant against [Dorothy] the wife of John Joardan of Blickling, labourer. She had lifted the door of William House woolcomber [of Blickling] off of the latch & stole a poke with wheat & was seen to go away with [it]. And when House did charge her with them, she threw him both [sic] again out of her doors.[330]
[f. 34r] *24⁰ 8bris 1665:* Robert Spurrell & Robert Short the two churchwardens of the parish of Thwaite did complain unto me that one [blank], being a young child, was within 40 days last past (that is on Friday last was 5 weeks) brought into a tenement in Thwaite aforesaid under the yearly value of £10 to be settled with one Henry Colby, whose wife was to be and now is its nurse, but what its name is, who be its parents, or whence it came, they know not, & that the said young child is likely to be chargeable to the said parish of Thwaite.
Eodem: James Risbrough bound to the peace upon Francis Balls's oath. See 20 [October].
Eodem: Thomas Allison, junior, constable de Ingworth pro Thomas Gay. 30 [October] Robert Grand pro Robert Overton.[331]
26 [October]: a warrant for Thomas Hind & Robert Berry, chosen at the leet, sworn constables of Banningham.
Eodem: William Grice & William Sexten, the two overseers[332] of the poor of the parish of Sustead (as Mr Blofield & William Ransome, the only churchwarden there the day before: see 30 [October]) made complaint unto me that Margaret White & her daughter did within 40 days last past (that is about 3 weeks since) come from the town house in Gresham in this county to settle in a tenement in Sustead aforesaid under the yearly value of £10 (that is of £4 10s.) with Goodwife Harwood, and that the said Margaret & her daughter be poor persons & likely to be chargeable to the said parish of Sustead, she having taken collection at Gresham already.
Eodem: a warrant against Nicholas Smith [bailiff of North Erpingham hundred] for suing Dennis Flaxman [husbandman of Felbrigg] when John

Cozens [husbandman of same], who had first bidden him & given him 4d., forthwith forbade him giving him the 4d. for himself, the agreement being made all at the same time & in Smith's view.[333]
27º [October]: Robert Berry & Thomas Hind sworn constables of Banningham.[334]
30 [October]: William Ransome only churchwarden of Sustead made like complaint of Margaret White & her daughter coming for [sic] Gresham to Sustead to settle with William Harwood, but they say she goeth monthly to Gresham where she lived in the poor house, as the overseers there made complaint on the 26th instant.
Eodem: Robert Grand sworn constable of Ingworth pro Robert Overton, per Oliver Neave & Thomas Townshend's warrant.[335]
31 [October]: a warrant against Thomas Allison for turning away Hannah Chapman his apprentice, keeping her clothes & threatening her.
Eodem: a general warrant against Thomas Hadin for assaulting & wounding John Bucke [one word illegible] of Aylsham, Hadin being Mrs Greenwood's brother & Bucke a watchman.
2 8bris [sic]: I joined with Sir John Palgrave in 2 warrants upon complaints made to him for removing William Purdy, his wife & five children to Holt, and Michael Wilson, his wife & children to Beeston-next-the-Sea from Gresham.
[f. 34v] *2 9bris 1665:* a warrant for [blank] Learner to be sworn constable of West Beckham, being chosen at Gresham leet.
Eodem: a warrant of assault & battery for John Howes, tailor [of Bayfield], & Thomas Wiggot, husbandman [of Blickling], for assaulting & beating Rice England (being Sir John Hobart's bailiff) in the highway causelessly.[336]
6 [November]: John Richman sworn constable of Colby instead of John Black, & Joshua Robinson is to be sworn instead of John Stoneham.
8 [November]: a general warrant against Thomas Allen the Aylsham bailiff upon complaint of Robert Priest of Briston.[337]
9 [November]: Joshua Robinson sworn constable of Colby.
11 [November]: a warrant to send Thomas Turner of Southrepps, labourer, to Aylsham Bridewell. He had taken a spade from Richard Ellys [gentleman of Southrepps] his stable door within his yard and said he meant to use it & return it again.[338]
13 [November]: a general warrant against Cecily Hooke of Sheringham upon complaint of Robert Barnard.
Eodem: Robert Webster sworn constable of Calthorpe instead of Richard Wegg. John Tubbing is the other new-chosen constable.
Eodem: a warrant for Robert Fisher of Felmingham to search for 12 ducks & 4 geese.[339]
27 [November]: William Trouse sworn constable of Wickmere instead of Thomas Flockden.
30 [November]: a general warrant against Elizabeth, wife of Anthony Cooke, miller, for scandalizing Mary Arger [wife of Robert Arger husbandman], all of Cromer, for a witch.[340]
4 December: a warrant for William Smith of Colby to pay John Witchingham the 17s. arrears of his wages of 30s. for 32 weeks ended last Michaelmas.

7 [December]: a warrant against Robert Sprunt of North Walsham for drawing & taking away one of the hooks of an hanged gate out of the tree of Robert Bond, Sir R. K. farmer in Antingham.[341]
10 [December]: a general warrant & to bring sureties for good behaviour against Robert Challis of Sheringham, who came from [Great] Yarmouth & I shut up, who threateneth to burn his wife's house to the hazarding Robert Cooke's, being next.
26 [December]: I sent Dorothy Joardan, the wife of William Joardan of Blickling, to the whipping. She had got wheat out of House his chamber.[342]
28 [December]: a general warrant against Robert Gedg, labourer, & Margaret Everard, spinster, both of Felmingham, whom he hath got with child.[343]

[fols. 35r-93v are blank]

[fols. 94r-v] 43 Elizabeth c. 2: An Act for the Relief of the Poor.[344]

NOTES TO THE TEXT

1. Before deletion the oath began 'Either of you for yourself'.
2. Before deletion the phrase read 'God respectively help either of you.'
3. Illegible words deleted.
4. The justices listed below may be identified respectively as Nicholas Stileman of Snettisham (1614-1683), Samuel Smythe of Colkirk (d. 1664), Simon Britiffe of Cley-next-the-Sea (c. 1625-1686), Edward Pepys of Brunsthorpe and South Creake (c. 1617-1663), and Nathaniel Shouldham of Kettlestone (c. 1625-1671). RD noted in the margin of this list 'I was sick', with brackets to indicate his comment applied to Michaelmas 1661, Twelfth-night 1662 and Easter 1662.
5. 'Simon' is written over 'Samuel' and 'Smith' is deleted.
6. See Appendix I.
7. Certificate of election, 6 August, Norfolk Record Office [hereafter 'NRO'], Aylsham 304. The designation 'NRO' is omitted from further references to the Aylsham collection.
8. Warrant, 16 July 1662, Aylsham 347. Flaxman beat Gilbert with a pair of tongs. See below 24 September 1662.
9. Warrant, Aylsham 347.
10. 'Armerys' is deleted.
11. Warrant, Aylsham 1, endorsed with RD's notes as below 15 August 1662. Elizabeth Kendall and Rose Watkins were also to appear.
12. Warrant, Aylsham 347.
13. E. Britift to RD, 14 August [1662], Aylsham 1, warned RD not to believe Dawson's complaints. On the letter is RD's draft warrant to distrain 20s. from Milles for allowing tippling. See informations of Dawson and Kendall, ibid.
14. Warrant, Aylsham 347.
15. 'Appear' is deleted.
16. 'Cause to come' deleted. Warrant, Aylsham 347. Alice Smith claimed Spurrell was of ill fame and behaviour.
17. Warrant, 28 August, Aylsham 1, for strict execution of previous warrants and to bring Mary and Robert Taylour of North Walsham to testify.
18. Warrant, Aylsham 347.
19. See below 4 March 1663. In January 1662 Gambling was suspected of barn breaking: papers dated 13 and 14 January 1662, Aylsham 347.
20. See above 11 August 1662.
21. Warrant, Aylsham 347.
22. Gyle vat, in which the wort is left to ferment in brewing.
23. Tyler's information, Aylsham 347. She said she lay only once with Massy. He, learning she was pregnant, offered to take her to London but then ignored her.
24. Damaged warrant, Aylsham 347, for Tuck's appearance on 15 October on charges brought by John Cockman and one Bell. See below 12 November 1663.

25. Draft warrant, Aylsham 304, notes that the dwelling was a fire hazard.
26. Warrant, Aylsham 347, describes Woolsey as late spinster. See examination of Smith (called a labourer), 29 October, Aylsham 304, admitting fornication with Woolsey in the house of Smith's former master, Robert Browne, clerk. Smith asked Woolsey to marry him before she was pregnant. John Smith and Thomas Catherine of Metton were each bound on 28 October in £10 for Smith's appearance at sessions, bonds released on the couple's marriage. R. Fawcit to RD, n.d., Aylsham 306, attests to the marriage.
27. RD's note of the swearing on the warrant concerning Samuel Smith, 28 October 1662 above.
28. Warrant, Aylsham 347. A memorandum from Augustine Thornton, steward of Beeston Priory Manor in Runton, 15 October, ibid., says that the two replaced Robert Feazar and Nicholas Dawson. See below 17 November 1662.
29. Warrant and examinations, Aylsham 347. Joyce said she lay with Simpson at Whitsun on Antingham common but hid her pregnancy fearing he would flee. Simpson denied intercourse with Joyce. See informations of Sarah, wife of Robert Bell, Ann wife of John Pratt, John Stowe, and John Thompson, butcher, all of Antingham, 18 January 1663, ibid. See below 10 March 1663.
30. Warrant, Aylsham 304. See above 6 November 1662.
31. Warrant, Aylsham 304.
32. Draft and warrant, with Sir John Palgrave, Aylsham 347. The latter document is scored through and endorsed 'suppress eodem'. See draft removal order to constables of Alby to return Bunne to Thwaite, Aylsham 193. Sir John Palgrave, kt. and 1st bart. of Norwood Barningham (1605-1672), was a member of the quorum, unlike RD. On Bunne see below 4 and 6 March 1663.
33. Warrant for appearance, 16 December, Aylsham 1, and draft warrant, with Sir John Palgrave, for committal on sheet with recognizance for Moyses and wife Elizabeth to appear against Clerke, ibid. See also informations of Clerke (noted as a former soldier in Col. Whalley's horse regiment), of Moyses (also given as Moyse and Moysis) and his wife, ibid. Clerke was charged with threatening the king's life and with blaming bishops for the country's former ruin and for 'the chimney money'. Clerke denied the charges, claiming that Moyses, for whom he worked as a tailor, feared that Clerke was taking away his customers. See RD's rough notes and four draft letters, ibid., where he explained that he had only charged Clerke with breach of the peace because he doubted the truth of Moyses's accusation, considering Moyses's delay in bringing a complaint, his suspicious behavior on examination, and the quarrel between him and Clerke. See also RD's draft letter to Justice Mathew Hale, n.d., on letter cover 'For Robert Doughty Esq. at his house at Hanworth,' Aylsham 347. Here RD said that Moyses, whom he had bound to assizes to prosecute Clerke, had gone to Holland. Clerke is named among the prisoners for gaol delivery at

Lent assizes 1663: quarter sessions rolls 1662-63, 1663-65, NRO, C/S3, Box 46.

34. The object is presumably a 'fall-gate', a gate across a public road. See notes for this warrant, naming John Drake as the victim, on verso of draft warrant to constables of Antingham, 2 January 1663, Aylsham 347.
35. Warrant, Aylsham 304, on complaint of Russels's mother, Sara Patrick.
36. Draft, Aylsham 347 and warrant, Aylsham 1, with Sir George Windham of Cromer, kt. (d. 1663), for Antingham to pay 10s. and wood, the 3s. weekly allowance being insufficient for the cost of the cure. E. De Grey to RD, 26 January 1663, Aylsham 1, called the Blackstons 'a pair of lazy, idle, slothful persons' unworthy of relief and asked RD to dismiss their complaint.
37. Notes and two warrants with Sir George Windham, Aylsham 347, for removing the parties in both cases. See also drafts on verso of sheet with removal order of 31 August 1665, Aylsham 304 and draft order for Becke, Aylsham 193.
38. Probably either Alby or Aldborough.
39. Draft warrant, Aylsham 347. Carr had been evicted by her brother, Stephen Durrant.
40. Warrant of 19 February with draft recognizance of 23 February for Duffield's appearance at sessions, Aylsham 347. 'W' may stand for Wickmere, not far from Thurgarton.
41. This entry is marked 'N' in the margin. The justice is Robert Baldock of Tacolneston (c. 1625-1691), knighted in 1671. The Twelfth-night sessions met at Little Walsingham on 22 January 1663.
42. Warrant of Jacob Preston, 23 February, Aylsham 347, for appearance of Gunner and Robert Gunner, yeoman, at petty sessions in North Walsham on 24 February.
43. See below 10 March 1663.
44. Informations of Robert Allen and Edward Woodrow of North Walsham, labourer, examination of Thomas Gambling and warrant to convey him, 4 March, Aylsham 347. Allen measured the thief's footprint, which fitted Gambling, who he said had been detected of barn robbing at the last two assizes. Gambling denied all, saying he had been ploughing. Woodrow implicated Bunne (given as a bricklayer) in the theft of oats from William Hogan of Roughton. See above 23 September 1662 and below 27 March, 21 May and 28 July 1663 and 5 May 1664. RD's draft to Justice Mathew Hale, n.d. (on a letter cover 'For Robert Doughty Esq. at his house at Hanworth,' Aylsham 347), contains RD's inquiry into the disposition at assizes of the charges against Gambling and Bunne.
45. Warrant, examinations of twelve individuals, bastardy order (and draft), Aylsham 347. The informants were Mary Joyce of Antingham, spinster; Elizabeth, wife of John Kirby; Margaret Plattyn; Mary Clarke; John Thompson, butcher, Mary Joyce's master; John Cockman and John Stowell of Antingham, worsted weavers; Robert Wagstafe of same; Lydia Tracy, widow; Mary

Pratt of Erpingham, spinster; Sara the wife of Robert Ball; and John Simpson, brother of Thomas. RD and Sir George Windham decided that Thomas Simpson was the father of Mary Joyce's child and ordered the two whipped. Joyce was to keep the child until age eight, when it would be apprenticed. Simpson was to be bound in £40 to pay 24s. immediate maintenance, 2s. per week for the first year, 18d. per week thereafter, and £5 when the child was apprenticed. See above 17 November 1662 and below 20 and 21 April 1663.

46. Warrant of this date and information of c. 3 April, Aylsham 347, on charges of Thomas Hind of Banningham, blacksmith, who traded a colt with John Cully of Trunch for a horse. Bunne took the colt, claiming Hind had not paid for the horse. See above 4 and 6 March 1663 and below 21 May and 28 July 1663 and 5 May 1664.

47. See below, misplaced entry for 24 April and 5 May 1663, after that of 29 May 1663. It is unclear why Spurrell's and Risebrough's names are in the margin here.

48. See above 10 March 1663. See also draft bond of 27 April, Aylsham 347, for payment of £5 6s. by Edmund Simpson, worsted weaver of Antingham and father of Thomas, to the parish of Antingham for the support of the child, unless the Simpsons provided 1s. per week for a year.

49. Paper headed 'Sherenham April the 21 1662' [but from 1663], Aylsham 347, with a list of 16 alehousekeepers, may relate to this meeting. See also three alehouse licenses, issued 21 April 1663, and a list of 20 alehousekeepers on verso of a certificate concerning petty constables of Norwood Barningham, 9 May 1663, ibid.

50. Draft conveyance order for Robert Bond [sic], on sheet headed 'Sherenham April the 21 1662'; draft order, 30 April, informing Weybourne of Aylmerton's appeal to sessions of RD's and Simon Brittif's removal order; and draft recognizance for the appearance of Aylmerton officers at sessions to appeal the order: all in Aylsham 347.

51. Presumably Burgh-next-Aylsham.

52. Warrant, Aylsham 347. See below 21 May 1663.

53. Warrant, Aylsham 347. Robert Humpfrey was also to testify.

54. Warrant, Aylsham 347.

55. The Poor Law Act of 1662, 14 Charles II, c. 12.

56. Warrant of 22 May, Aylsham 1, for Bunne's appearance on 28 May. RD's notes indicate that Thwaite's constables, Robert Short and John Lubbock, went to Bunne on 25 May and found him averse to appear before any JP but Sir Thomas Rant of Thorpe Market, kt. (1606-1671). Since neither Bunne nor Colby's officers gave security to Thwaite, RD and Palgrave ordered Bunne's removal to Colby. This may be the same Bunne noted above 27 March 1663 and below 5 May 1664.

57. See above 6 May 1663; memorandum of release, 20 May, Aylsham 347.

58. Warrant with Sir John Palgrave, Aylsham 347, for Marys's

appearance at next sessions 'for the hundred of North Erpingham', endorsed with testimony on the beating. See Palgrave's warrant of 22 May, Aylsham 1, for the appearance as witnesses of Judith wife of 'old' Evered, limeburner, Mary wife of William Wells, and Thomas Caudron and wife, all of Metton.

59. Warrant of 24 April with Sir John Palgrave, Aylsham 347, for Dyball to show cause why they should not be removed; draft warrant of 5 May, ibid., on sheet headed 'Sherenham April the 21 1662,' to convey the Dyballs to the Aylsham house of correction as vagabonds, they having ignored the former warrant.

60. Warrant, Aylsham 347.

61. Warrant, Aylsham 347, for Crow's appearance at next sessions 'for our hundred of North Erpingham'.

62. Warrant with Sir John Palgrave, Aylsham 347, for Town Barningham officers to give security for Grey or show why he should not be sent there from Bessingham.

63. Warrant of 15 June, Aylsham 347.

64. Warrant, Aylsham 347, with RD's notes that Smith claimed his wife sold beer while he was away, that this was Riches's first conviction and that Bun admitted selling four barrels of beer he bought off J. Hewitt of Aylsham at 14s. per barrel. See below 27 June 1663.

65. Warrant, Aylsham 1, notes that the constables could not levy distress against Riches, being unable to distinguish her goods from her mother's.

66. The reference to Tuesday could apply to the next entry.

67. Warrant, Aylsham 347, noting that John Beacon, bricklayer of Knapton, said he worked on Mileham's oven and chimney with bricks he had formerly used to top the church wall.

68. Warrant, Aylsham 347.

69. Warrant, Aylsham 347.

70. A paper, 7 August 1663, Aylsham 347, indicates that Ann Durrant made the threats after a quarrel with her landlady Green. Green had RD's warrant suspended, and RD then got Ann Durrant to agree to leave Green's house by 16 August and pay Green 11s.

71. Warrant, Aylsham 347.

72. William Burleigh was clerk of the peace. The reference is presumably to *The Reports of Sir George Croke...*, 3 parts, London, 1657-1661.

73. This entry is inserted above the preceding one. See warrant of 28 July, Bunne's examination of 29 July (with draft recognizance for Hobbys's appearance against Bunne) and Hobbys's examination, n.d., Aylsham 347; also draft warrant, Aylsham 1. Bunne, also described as a mason, denied taking the horse but gave a suspicious account of his actions and whereabouts. Hobbys suspected him as one who 'liveth idly & is son-in-law to one Gam- bling who hath been an old thief.' On this pair see above 23 September 1662 and 4, 6 and 27 March 1663 and below 5 May 1664.

74. See above 9 July 1663, where the name is given as Corb.

75. Warrant, Aylsham 347, noting that Riches appeared on 8 August, having paid the 20s. fine. She was discharged but warned for the future.
76. See below 17 August 1663.
77. Scrap of notes concerning this and the following entry, Aylsham 347. See above 15 August 1663.
78. Warrant of 21 August, Aylsham 347, for Erpingham to show why Mathew, Mary and Susan Brett should not be settled there; draft of 24 August, ibid., ordering that the three children of the late John Brett should receive 3d. apiece per week maintenance from Thurgarton, their mother having remarried John Bell of Thurgarton. Sir Thomas Rant, kt., of Thorpe Market (1606-1671) was a member of the quorum, unlike RD.
79. Warrant and recognizances, Aylsham 347. See below 25 August 1663. The justice referred to is Oliver Neave of Great Witchingham (c. 1601-1679).
80. Warrant, Aylsham 347.
81. Warrants, Aylsham 347. Hating the father and Robert Crowe, brazier, stood surety.
82. Warrant, Aylsham 347.
83. Warrant, Aylsham 304.
84. Warrant, Aylsham 347. Doaghty is described as a tailor of Northrepps.
85. Warrant, Aylsham 347. See below 16 November 1663.
86. Warrant, Aylsham 347.
87. See Appendix I.
88. Long Stratton.
89. Warrant, Aylsham 347, gives Frost as a husbandman. Whight or White was earlier apprehended on a warrant of Sir John Palgrave. Nicholls got away with the help of Davy, who threatened Frost, prompting RD's warrant. See also warrant of 19 October, with recognizance of Frost and T. Buthell, miller, both of Gresham, bound to press the indictment against White and Nicholls: Aylsham 347. See below 15 January 1665.
90. Warrant, Aylsham 347. Empson was bound in £20 and Robert Russells, gentleman, and John Soame, barber, both of Aylsham, in £10 apiece.
91. Warrant, Aylsham 1, notes that Haylett and Thomas Smith were bound in £20 each to keep the peace.
92. 'N' in the margin.
93. Warrant, Aylsham 347, where RD noted that Tuck told Bell, 'You Bell kiss my arse & tell Justice Doughty I said so.' See above 14 October 1662. RD, Sir John Palgrave and Sir George Windham had suppressed Tuck's alehouse by warrant of 11 May 1663. In 1664 she received a licence: see certificate recommending her, 31 May 1664, Aylsham 347, and below 30 May 1665.
94. Warrant, Aylsham 347. William Coxton and William Primrose were to testify. See above 28 September and below 18 November 1663.
95. Warrant, Aylsham 347, endorsed with informations of 20 November

by Bacon, William Snelling of Dilham, linen weaver, Stephen Greene of Crostwick, husbandman, and Robert Fisher of Felmingham, yeoman and constable.

96. Draft warrant and warrant, informations of George Ebbetts of North Walsham, butcher, and James Stubs of Felmingham, husbandman, and warrant of 20 November to convey the Starkys to Norwich gaol for want of sureties: all in Aylsham 347. Draft warrant to commit, 21 November, Aylsham 1. See below 16 December 1663.

97. Certificate of 2 November for Black to come and be sworn, Aylsham 347.

98. Draft, on certificate of 23 November 1663, and warrant, Aylsham 347, noting that RD on 25 November ordered Leasy to pay Flatfoote 22s. more.

99. Warrant, Aylsham 347.

100. A tree or shrub of the willow family.

101. Warrant of 15 December, Aylsham 347, to gaol the Starkys until they gave surety to keep the peace towards Thomas Bacon of Dilham and Stephen Greene of Crostwick-next-Didlington, husbandman. See above 17 and 18 November 1663.

102. Warrant of this date, and informations of 23 December of Robert Fisher, yeoman, and Robert Martill, worsted weaver, both of Felmingham, Aylsham 347. Fisher said RD's warrant only extended to William Starky, not his wife, and argued 'that it was not law to examine the one part & not the other.'

103. 'Did' is deleted.

104. 'Many' is deleted.

105. Informations, Aylsham 347, of Mary, wife of William Smith, yeoman of Blickling, and of Sara Williams and James Cooper, Smith's servants, indicating that John Smith threatened Mary Smith.

106. Two illegible words deleted.

107. Warrant, Aylsham 347, endorsed with informations of 30 December and 1 January of Dyony Lound and the constables, implicating Lound's father, Michael Scholler, in the purported theft.

108. Warrant, Aylsham 1, with note of Fuller's confession; see below 7 January 1664.

109. Warrant, Aylsham 347, noting that Abs was sworn the same day. But see below 7 January 1664.

110. 'Colby' is deleted.

111. Warrant of 7 January, Aylsham 347, endorsed with certificate of 25 January that St. Augustine officials were to appear in this matter and with a certificate that Yell's son Thomas was baptized in St. Augustine's on 4 October 1660.

112. 'Thursday' is deleted.

113. 'Sojourner' is deleted.

114. 'Town' is deleted.

115. 'N' in the margin. Draft warrant, Aylsham 347.

116. See above 22 December 1663.

117. Draft recognizance on letter from Sir J. Palgrave to RD, 15 January

1664, Aylsham 1. See above 24 October 1663.

118. 'Of the' is deleted.
119. See below 8 February 1664.
120. See above 22 December 1663.
121. See above 6 February 1664.
122. Warrant of 1 March, with note of appearance on 3 March, Aylsham 347.
123. See above 8 January 1664.
124. Undated examination of Margaret White, Aylsham 347, indicating that her husband Henry had been gone two years. In October 1663 she lay with Cubitt, who promised to maintain her and any child she might have. Cubitt denied the child and refused to help.
125. 'At' is deleted.
126. Warrant with note of the conviction, and informations of 23 March from Greene, Henry Spall and Mary Lamb, Aylsham 347. Greene originally said he would draw ten barrels more. Before RD he admitted having drawn 4½ barrels but only for workmen and his family.
127. 'They' is deleted.
128. Warrants of 12 and 13 April, Aylsham 347. RD rescinded his warrant after learning details. When Jezebel's son Mathew had a quarrel while gambling, she intervened, and Henry Allen and Miles Purgall beat her, Allen threatening to 'mark her for a witch.' Constable Nicholas Fisher blamed Miles Purgall and Allen. RD saw signs of 'blows & bruises' on Jezebel, noting also the words aimed at her, 'Go suckle your imps, go show your marks.'
129. Jacob Preston of Beeston (1614-1683). See his warrant, 21 April, Aylsham 347, with RD's note of taking recognizances on 25 March [sic]. See below 6 July 1664.
130. Draft warrant, Aylsham 347, says Strunt.
131. Warrant, Aylsham 347, noting that Richard Allen and Dennis Flaxman were sworn on 27 April 1664: see below. Certificate of election, 25 April, ibid.
132. Warrant, Aylsham 347. Margaret and William Ransome were also to testify. RD noted that when ordered to pay the damages Rodgers 'forthwith borrowed the same of me.' Blofield did not accept the money as full recompense but took nothing more, since Rodgers was poor.
133. Warrant of this date and Bennington's information 6 May, Aylsham 347. Bunne said he got the rope from his father-in-law Thomas Gambling; Bennington was bound in £10, Roger Colby and Timothy Puxly in £5 apiece. See above 23 September 1662, 4, 6, 27 March, 5 May and 28 July 1663 for Bunne and Gambling.
134. Warrant, Aylsham 347. Shale blamed his wife for the theft. See below 5 July 1664.
135. Warrant, Aylsham 347.
136. Examinations of both parties, Aylsham 347. Lennow, with a wife and children at Mattishall, had drunk at Margetson's mother's alehouse with Mathew Cooke, whom Lennow accused of 'carnal

embracements' with Margetson. Margetson, who had a prior bastard, charged this child to Lennow.

137. Warrant, Aylsham 347.
138. Warrant against Underwood, Aylsham 1. See above 11 May 1664.
139. Certificate of election, 4 May 1664, Aylsham 347.
140. Warrant, Aylsham 347. See draft order for Bell to be whipped and fettered for one month as an idle person: Aylsham 304.
141. See below 4 July 1664.
142. Warrant, Aylsham 347, noting that on 9 June Kid received 12d. in satisfaction.
143. Draft warrant, Aylsham 347.
144. Warrant, Aylsham 347. Harris's servant Rose Pratt was also to appear.
145. Warrant, Aylsham 347; draft, Aylsham 193. Morgan with a drawn weapon attacked Nicholas Smith of Gresham, husbandman and bailiff of North Erpingham hundred. Smith complained to Skelton, who commended Morgan. RD was told that Skelton and Morgan had gone to London. See below 25 July 1664.
146. Warrant, Aylsham 347. 'Bromewell' is perhaps Broomholm.
147. Warrant, Aylsham 347, endorsed with terms of agreement noted below after the entries of 29 June 1664.
148. Warrant, NRO, Hamond deposit 21.8.75, 'Documents from Le Neve/Blomefield collections,' S 116 C. See warrant of 7 June 1664 to the constables of Thurgarton and Sustead for the appearance of Thomas Copeman to answer charges of William Grice of Sustead: ibid.
149. Warrant, Aylsham 347, noting two instances of fraud.
150. Warrant, Aylsham 347, gives Colke. See above 9 May and below 30 July 1664.
151. 'Of' is deleted.
152. Draft warrant to convey the children, Aylsham 347. See below 9 July 1664.
153. Lansdale's release of Newland, 4 July (see above 31 May 1664) and Slayter's release of Riches, 6 July (see above 25 April 1664), Aylsham 347.
154. 'He' is deleted.
155. Informations of Cley and Rix, Aylsham 347. See below 9 July 1664.
156. Warrant, Aylsham 347. Ann, wife of Benjamin Grandger of Blickling, husbandman, was assaulted by James Smith.
157. 'Eodem' is deleted.
158. See above 5 July 1664.
159. See certificate, 11 September 1664, Aylsham 347, from Edmund Wharton, vicar of Worstead, that Rix and Sara Cley were married as ordered. See above 7 July 1664.
160. Warrant, Aylsham 347, requires Susan Webb and Mary Wilson to appear.
161. A solid line is drawn across the page here.
162. The justices not previously identified are Francis Bacon of Norwich (c. 1624-1692); Robert Longe of Reymerston (1619-1688); and

Francis Corey (or Corye) of Bramerton (c. 1596-1678).

163. Sir William Doyly of Shotesham, kt. and 1st bart. (1614-1677).
164. 'Whose' is deleted.
165. See RD's undated notes, Aylsham 1 and Aylsham 347.
166. Warrant with RD's endorsement of the swearing, Aylsham 347.
167. Warrant, Aylsham 347, giving Grice as a labourer. RD notes that on 23 July the three women confessed before him. Being their first offences, they were allowed to make satisfaction and paid down 4d. each.
168. Warrant, Aylsham 347. See above 23 June 1664.
169. Draft and warrant, Aylsham 347.
170. 'Dobson' is deleted.
171. See above 5 July 1664.
172. A double line is drawn through the text here.
173. See Appendix I.
174. 'Croke's Car' may refer to that part of *Croke's Reports* covering the reign of Charles I: see *The Reports of Sir George Croke, knight...revised and published in English by Sir Harebotle Grimston*, London, 1657.
175. 'Wife' is deleted. The justices noted here and not previously identified are Sir Nicholas L'Estrange of Hunstanton, 3rd bart. (1632-1669); Sir Edward Walpole of Houghton, KB (1622-1668); Roger Spelman of Holme-next-the-Sea (1625-1678); Henry Clifton of Toftrees (c. 1618-1670); Sir Thomas Guybon of Thursford, kt. (1612-1666); and Samuel Harsnett of Great Fransham (d. 1670).
176. A line is drawn through the text here.
177. 'Her' is deleted.
178. Palgrave's warrant, 8 August, Aylsham 347. Palmer, servant of Samuel Yaxley, husbandman of Weybourne, and Martha his wife, was accused of stealing linen and handkerchiefs: see Martha's undated information, ibid. See also S. Brittif's warrant of 12 August 1664 for appearance of Samuel and John Yaxley, accused by Robert Dix of Hevingham of forging a warrant from Brittif which charged Palmer with theft.
179. Warrant, Aylsham 347 describes Cutting as of Ingworth.
180. 'Did' is deleted.
181. 'The' is deleted.
182. 'Which is' is deleted.
183. Warrant, Aylsham 347, endorsed with informations of 29 August and ordering Winifred Wilson and Mary Marshall widows of Ingworth to appear. Wilson said Grime beat his wife, and Marshall said Grime had violently demanded ale of her. Welles (or Wellons) said Grime had been bound to keep the peace but now drove off her swine and threatened her. William Winnow, constable of Ingworth, said Grime refused to appear when ordered. RD noted that Mr Ransom questioned RD's jurisdiction, Ingworth being 'out of my limit, whereas my limit is throughout the county of Norfolk and this warrant was as general.' See below 29 August 1664.
184. Warrant, Aylsham 347. See above 26 August and below 1 Sep-

tember 1664.
185. Thomas Townshend of Lincoln's Inn and Horstead (c. 1608-1682).
186. See above 29 August 1664.
187. See below 8-9 September.
188. Warrant, Aylsham 347. See below 15 September 1664. Fisher is given as a husbandman of Suffield.
189. Palgrave's warrant, 3 September 1664, Aylsham 347. See above 1 September 1664.
190. Warrant, Aylsham 347, endorsed by RD that Cooper was sent to bridewell for a month.
191. See below 3 October 1664.
192. See above 9 September 1664.
193. Corye and RD were related through the Houghton family.
194. Warrant, Aylsham 347, calling Hooke 'spinster' and requiring Thomas Cooper the younger also to appear.
195. A second 'told' is deleted.
196. See above 29 September 1664.
197. Warrant, 7 October, Aylsham 347. A superscript '2' is placed over Martha Hay's name and a '1' over Robert Hay's name. '8bris' is written in the margin.
198. Warrant of 20 October, Aylsham 1, by RD and Sir John Palgrave at complaint of John Willis of West Beckham, worstedweaver.
199. Information of Slaughter, Aylsham 347. She yielded to Loveday, who promised to marry her if he did her wrong. Slaughter was afraid to tell Loveday of her pregnancy, hearing he had said 'If I meet with her, I will give her a kick or two & make her cast her calf.'
200. Certificate, 19 October, Aylsham 1, gives the name as Springall.
201. Certificate, 26 October, Aylsham 193.
202. 'Did' is deleted.
203. See below 21 July 1665.
204. Warrant, Aylsham 347, gives Thirkle; see below, where RD mistakenly repeats this entry, spelling the name thus.
205. Warrant, Aylsham 347.
206. See note on verso of certificates from churchwardens and overseers of Colby, 5 November 1664, Aylsham 347.
207. Warrant of Sir Jacob Astley, 7 November 1664, authorizing attachment by George, John and Henry Sprunt and Henry Starkey, bailiffs, of the goods of Susanna Davy, widow, by action of William Starkey, unless she made payment due to William Starkey by the next quarter sessions on 5 November [sic]: Aylsham 347. Certificate from William Annyson to RD, 24 November, suggests that since the error in it was minor, the warrant for seizure upon which the bailiffs had acted was valid: ibid.
208. This entry is bracketed in the margin.
209. Warrant, Aylsham 347, requires William Brettingham the younger to appear.
210. Perhaps Gorleston.
211. Informations, 27 December 1664, Aylsham 347, of Dorothy Benington of Alby, widow, Thomas Platting of same husbandman

and servant to John Benington, William Stubbs of Alby, and John Bishop of Thwaite, cordwainer. Thomas Platting and John, son of Dorothy Benington, fought with Bun and his wife Ann over trees Bun felled on property he rented from Bennington in Alby. Bun may be the suspected thief Samuel Bunne from the neighbouring parish of Colby: see above 5 May 1664.

212. Warrant, Aylsham 347.
213. Two illegible names are deleted at the beginning of this entry.
214. See release of surety, 3 April 1665, Aylsham 347. Warrant, 19 October 1665, Aylsham 347, requires the appearance of Cooper and of Rose Pratt of Alby to answer misdemeanour charges by John Harris.
215. See below 22 February 1665.
216. See Palgrave to RD, 21 and 28 January 1665, British Library, Additional MS 27967, fols. 76-77v and Aylsham 193, respectively. Coo (also given as Coe) was gaoled after John Ellys, another of Palgrave's servants, deposed that Coo had been dancing at his father Nicholas's house.
217. See Palgrave to RD, 28 January 1665, Aylsham 193. The licence was for the family of James De Grey of Merton, Esq., JP and Palgrave's brother-in-law.
218. See below 22 March 1665.
219. Warrant, Aylsham 347.
220. Warrant, Aylsham 1, endorsed with informations of 6 February by John Rose, John Balls and the constable James Grey, indicating that Allen broke a window and abused Risbrough. Allen's wife wanted to pay for the window, but Risbrough insisted on sending for the constable. See below 14 February 1665.
221. Warrant, Aylsham 347.
222. Warrant, Aylsham 347. Endorsed with information of Thomas Lilly and Robert Graves, husbandmen of Runton, testifying to the unlicensed sale of ale by Platten (given as Platting) and Anfillis Lacy. Platten's son appeared and confessed the sale. See below 10 February 1665.
223. Undated information of Ann Rust, widow, Aylsham 347, who saw Williams come to Pooley's house with a whole gate. Williams said it was a small gate of William Empson's. See above 8 February and below 31 May 1665.
224. See above 9 February 1665.
225. See below 16 October 1665.
226. Memorandum, Aylsham 347, giving Risbrough as spinster. See above 31 January and 6-7 February 1665.
227. Warrant from Sir John Palgrave, 21 February 1665, Aylsham 1, ordering Widow Thoulder and Ann Thoulder also to appear and with RD's note that Berston and Wilson 'brought pork'.
228. 'Wool' is deleted.
229. See above 21 January 1665 and also R. Flynt, minister at Runton, to RD, 17 February 1665, Aylsham 190; RD's notes on verso of Flynt to RD, 27 May 1665, Aylsham 347; A. Thornton to RD, 12

July 1665, Aylsham 193; and Flynt to RD, [late] July 1665, Aylsham 193. Clerke and Abs apparently brought a trial against Pull (who had been wounded at sea fighting the Dutch) at summer assizes in 1665, causing him the expense of attending but then failing to appear themselves.

230. Warrant, Aylsham 347. See informations, ibid., of Everitt, Crosby, Thomas Causton (Crosby's servant) and John Money, butcher of Sustead. They indicate that Everitt (also given as a limeburner) had stolen fowl and felled an ash belonging to John Windham Esq., for which RD had Everitt pay restitution.

231. Warrant against Christopher Doughty, Aylsham 347.

232. Warrant, Aylsham 347.

233. Heather.

234. Warrant, Aylsham 347, with RD's endorsement that on 25 March Eades, miller of Cromer, returned to him and said the parties were agreed.

235. 'Of' is deleted.

236. Informations, 31 March and 21 April, Aylsham 347 of Mary Balderston, Margery Ellys the midwife, Elizabeth wife of William Dixon, lathriver (Balderston's mother), David Bloy and Jane Balls. Balderston (also Barderston and Balston), spinster of Sustead, named Robert Underwood of Gresham, gentleman, as the father. She later denied this, but it was confirmed by Margaret wife of William Ransom, Jane wife of William Harwood, Mary wife of William Barnes and Ellen wife of David Bloy. On 21 April Balderston came before RD and again named Underwood, whom she said had agreed, before RD made a bastardy order, to give her £5 maintenance. See above 31 January 1665.

237. Warrant, Aylsham 347, notes that a Mr Porter told RD that Rice's wife had an estate of £12, which the officers of Suffield wanted expended before they contributed to the couple's maintenance.

238. Warrant, Aylsham 347, endorsed by RD 'parties agreed'.

239. R. Flynt wrote RD, 12 April 1665, Aylsham 193, that he had ordered the cow (comprising the entire estate of widow Phillips [given as Philipson]) to be cared for by Cooke, who was to give Phillips 7d. per week and dwelling in his house. After Phillips complained of Cooke's treatment, Flynt ordered the cow to be wintered with Sara Pull, giving Cooke 16s. to release the bargain, although Cooke now falsely claimed to have the use of the cow until Mayday. Flynt said the entire village disliked Cooke.

240. Warrant, Aylsham 347, orders Robert Breese also to appear. See also R. Flynt to RD, 12 and 17 April 1665, Aylsham 193, concerning the preceding three entries.

241. Warrant, Aylsham 347. Grice and his servant Amy Mack informed RD that Nichols became abusive after consuming beer at Grice's house and when ejected had broken the window with a brick.

242. Warrant, Aylsham 347, notes that Rivett agreed to return Audrey Elwood's money. See also warrant of 13 April 1665 from Sir John Palgrave, ibid.

243. Warrant, Aylsham 347. Cooke was named in childbirth by Mary Reynolds of Witton but said he did not know if he had lain with her. He was bound in £10, his mother Anne Cooke and Robert Bently in £5 each: see below 24 April 1665.
244. See above 22 April and below 15 May 1665.
245. Warrant, Aylsham 347, notes that William Ransome, husbandman, was sworn on 10 May 1665: see below.
246. Warrant, British Library, Additional MS 27967, f. 78.
247. Draft, Aylsham 1 and warrant, British Library, Additional MS 27967, f. 79, noting that the default 'is of ill example'. See certificate by six men of Sheringham, including the curate, asking clemency for Miller, who had been left by her husband: ibid., f. 80.
248. 'Between' is deleted.
249. Warrant of 6 May, Aylsham 347.
250. Warrant, Aylsham 193.
251. See above 29 April 1665.
252. Warrant, Aylsham 347.
253. Warrant, Aylsham 347, and informations of Richardson and Coe, 10 and 11 May respectively. Richardson claimed Coe had lain with her three times and promised marriage each time; Coe, described as husbandman, denied the entire matter. See RD's undated draft warrant ordering Coe's release from gaol, on verso of warrant of 1 February 1665 against Margaret Bell, ibid.
254. Draft, Aylsham 347 and warrant, Aylsham 1, which latter describes Coates as Ann or Thomasine of Hevingham, current wife of Roger Flower. See above 10 May and below 5 July 1665.
255. Crayfish.
256. A wicker hamper.
257. Warrant, Aylsham 347, orders Peter Corke also to appear.
258. See R. Flynt, J. Warde, J. Woodrowe and T. Smith to RD, 5 June 1665, Aylsham 193, asking RD to release Richardson because he had fallen ill and would otherwise die. See above 22 May 1665.
259. Warrant, Aylsham 1.
260. 'Find' is deleted.
261. Corye's warrant, 22 May 1665, Aylsham 347, for appearance of Elizabeth Annison to be bound to good behaviour at the complaint of Anne Burghill of Aylsham, widow.
262. Undated draft on verso of warrant of the peace, 25 May 1665, Aylsham 1, against Ann Burrell and Mary Yarne.
263. 'William Fisher' is deleted.
264. 'Eodem' in the margin is deleted.
265. In the margin: 'Martha is her name'.
266. Examination of Reynolds, Aylsham 347.
267. Warrant, Aylsham 347, with RD's notes as below 10 June 1665.
268. See above 10 May 1665.
269. Perhaps 'pique'.
270. Warrant, Aylsham 347.
271. 'Yester[day]' is deleted.
272. 'That end' deleted.

273. Warrant, Aylsham 1, calls Branding 'an abuser & contemner of authority.' RD noted that the parties were agreed 'as themselves told me.' See above 9 and below 12 June 1665.
274. Warrant of 10 June, Aylsham 347. See below 12 June 1665.
275. Information of Elizabeth Dixon, Aylsham 193, says that Everett, claiming to have bought the veal at Holt market, gave her some to pay a debt. When Bond and the constable Ransom approached, Everett fled.
276. Draft order, 9 June 1665, Aylsham 347, for Barwick to pay Webster 3s. for hearth tax and for Webster to return to Barwick his distrained goods. The 3s. was for three hearths; Webster demanded for four, but RD and Sir John Palgrave discharged Bar- wick from the fourth, after their personal inspection found it decayed.
277. Certificate to this effect to the constables of Swanton Abbot, Aylsham 347. See above 9 and 10 June 1665.
278. Warrant, Aylsham 347, with RD's endorsement that 'the parties are agreed'.
279. Warrant, Aylsham 347, orders William Calk also to appear. See below 26 June 1665.
280. 'Crown' is deleted.
281. Starky, sitting nearby, challenged Marfield for saying the words and later made them known to others. Marfield denied speaking them. The two had recently fallen out: Marfield held goods of Starky in pawn, and Starky had threatened to get even with him: informations, 16 June 1665, Aylsham 1.
282. Pinafore.
283. Warrant, Aylsham 347.
284. Warrant, Aylsham 1, with RD's notes indicating that Robert Custance and John Neale of the town told him that Coe had been in the town house for the poor, owned by William Custance, but that it became so decayed Coe went to the parsonage. See draft of undated warrant, Aylsham 347.
285. See RD's undated paper, Aylsham 347, noting that Eastwick, taken while begging at Wickmere Hall, confessed to being unsettled for four years past.
286. Warrant, Aylsham 347. RD notes that Buttivant knocked Barnie's wife, Susan Herring, unconscious for a quarter hour.
287. Warrant, Aylsham 347.
288. Warrant, Aylsham 347, at the complaint of Thomas, father of John Reive. See above 13 June 1665. A draft of this warrant appears on verso of a warrant of 9 June 1665, Aylsham 347, for the appearance of Thomas Rising.
289. Warrant, Aylsham 1; see above 15 June 1665. William Starky's information, 29 June, ibid., notes that when questioned about his purportedly treasonable words Marfield replied, 'Will, you have got a cup many times & so may I. And a word may slip out of a man's mouth more than he is aware of and now I am like to be apprehended.' RD's undated notes, ibid., indicate that Mr Williamson, constable of Felmingham, asked RD if William Starky

was bound to sessions to prosecute Marfield. RD said that because only one man had heard Marfield's words (and he not an unimpeachable witness), and because RD could not consult with another justice as to whether the words were treasonable, RD had only bound Marfield to his good behaviour. RD told the Starkys that if they went to sessions, Marfield might be bound to assizes for speaking treasonable words, but RD did not bind them to appear.

290. Warrant, 3 July 1665, British Library, Additional MS 27967, f. 85. Brook was charged with breaking into the chamber of Elizabeth Pierson and her husband and threatening to pull them out of bed.

291. Warrant, Aylsham 304.

292. Immoral.

293. Warrant, Aylsham 347, with verso endorsement of informations of 8 July of Stephen Smith of Thorpe Market, tailor, and Ann Powle of same, daughter of Powle the mason (also described as Powle the smith). Walby told Smith that she and the other two women were with Amis while gathering strawberries.

294. See below 14 July 1665.

295. See below 22 July 1665.

296. Undated draft warrants, Aylsham 1.

297. Undated draft warrants, Aylsham 1, where Beatrice is given as the wife of Thomas Challeng.

298. Undated draft warrant and removal orders, Aylsham 347. The order made by RD and Sir John Palgrave (see above 27 October 1664) was confirmed upon appeal at sessions, 13 April 1665: see quarter sessions order book, NRO, C/S2/2.

299. 'The' is deleted.

300. See above 14 July 1665. Informations of Priscilla Argent and of Thomas Priest and Thomas Gambling, constables of same, 24 July, Aylsham 347, indicate that Lomb tried to coerce the con- stables into taking Argent to bridewell for being out of service, despite a certificate from RD and Sir John Palgrave that she had been hired by James Jempson of Itteringham. Lomb disparaged the certificate as coming from two justices 'out of the limit', and said that if Argent was to be hired, it must be before justice Oliver Neave.

A note of fines, fees and sessions orders headed 'Fakenham sessions July 1665' includes an entry for 'the attachment against Mr Lombe de [blank] for words against Mr Doughty, viz, Though you be a justice of peace yet you do not speak true': 'Accounts 1660-1676', NRO, Norfolk quarter sessions uncatalogued papers, material from Norwich city records, case 22, shelf a (4). RD was absent from the sessions held at Little Walsingham on 12 October 1665 when Lomb appeared on Oliver Neave's warrant to answer charges: quarter sessions session book, NRO, C/S1/8. The ultimate disposition of the case is not noted.

301. Altered from 'Margaret'.

302. Warrant, Aylsham 347.

303. See Roberts's release of Stanton's surety, 9 August 1665, Aylsham 347.

304. This entry is scored through, but see 4 August 1665 below.
305. Draft warrant on a sheet with a draft warrant against Thomas Starky of Felmingham (see below 25 August 1665), and damaged warrant, both Aylsham 347, for the appearance of Elizabeth Swan, Susan Dickthorne and Mary Beare on complaint of Edward Rye of Cromer, butcher. The warrant is endorsed with RD's partly-illegible notes of his interrogation, 4 August 1665 below.
306. 'Page' is deleted.
307. Warrant, Aylsham 347.
308. Warrant of 3 August, Aylsham 347, describes Wilson as a comber of Beeston Regis, charged by John Bullimer with neglecting to teach Williams, an orphan, the mystery of combing. RD noted an agreement of 4 August for Bullimer to take the boy as apprentice and give Wilson the use of land worth 28s. per annum.
309. Informations, 14 August 1665, Aylsham 347, of Susan wife of Robert Barnes of Blickling, gardener, Elizabeth wife of Christopher Reynolds of same, labourer, and Thomas Springall of same, worsted weaver, suggest that Elizabeth Grand, who was pregnant, had called Ann Granger a drunken whore and old jade. The informants questioned whether Granger actually hit Grand with a stick.
310. Warrant, 13 August, Aylsham 347.
311. See below 30 August 1665.
312. Warrant, 14 August, Aylsham 347.
313. Warrant, Aylsham 1, indicates confusion between two different fighting cocks, one of which Webster apparently obtained in trade from one Robert Catherine and claimed to have sold to Nathaniel Stolleday, draper of Walsham. Webster and his mother gave different accounts concerning the matter.
314. Undated draft warrant, Aylsham 347, on sheet with draft of warrant for three pease stealers in Cromer: see above 2 August 1665. A dike's holl is a ditch. Thomas Starky in turn accused his daughter-in-law of obtaining the warrant to drive him from his house, knowing he could not find surety.
315. Warrant, Aylsham 347, requires Mary Tilney of Southrepps, widow, who lived with Henry King of same, to appear on charges brought by Mary, wife of William Bowing of same, carpenter.
316. See above 13 August 1665.
317. 'Lawrence' is deleted.
318. Draft removal order, Aylsham 304, on sheet with drafts of orders of 27 January and 9 February 1663.
319. Warrant, 4 September, Aylsham 347, with RD's note of sureties taken from the two Moyses. See release of surety by Peter Haw, 2 October 1665, Aylsham 347.
320. Warrant, Aylsham 347, with Otty's testimony. See 26-27, 29 September and 2 October 1665 below.
321. Warrant, Aylsham 347. Parker was turned away without her money after Margetson's wife quarreled with and beat her. See below 16 October 1665.
322. See below 2 October 1665.

323. 'With her grandfather there' is deleted.
324. Warrant, Aylsham 347, requiring Tobias Butcher the elder to appear and noting the parties' words as in the next entry.
325. Warrant for the appearance of Shepheard, Aylsham 347 and warrant for the appearance of Well, Aylsham 1.
326. 'Or householders in the house of' is deleted.
327. Warrant, Aylsham 347. See also the information of Ann Pye, given as spinster of Gresham, 16 October, Aylsham 1.
328. See above 14 February 1665.
329. See above 25 September 1665.
330. Warrant, 21 October, Aylsham 347, with RD's notes that Susan House, wife of William, denied she had given Dorothy Joardan permission to take the wheat. RD ordered Joardan taken to bridewell to be whipped and discharged: see below 26 December 1665.
331. Warrant of 24 October, from Thomas Townshend and Oliver Neave for the appearance of Allison and Grand to be sworn constables of Ingworth, endorsed by RD that he swore Allison on 25 and Grand on 30 October: Aylsham 1. See below 30 October 1665.
332. 'Churchwardens' is deleted.
333. Undated draft, Aylsham 347.
334. Certificate, 25 October, Aylsham 193. See above 26 October 1665.
335. See above 24 October 1665.
336. Warrant, Aylsham 1 and draft on verso of a letter from H. Carter to RD, 20 October 1665, Aylsham 193. Warrant of 3 November, Aylsham 347, for the appearance of Howes the younger (described as a seaman of Blickling) and of Thomas Wiggot. See informations taken, 3 November, Aylsham 1, from Richard Callow of Blickling, husbandman, Rice England and John Middleton, mole catcher, which note that the accused men failed to appear before RD. The informants testified that Howes, encouraged by Wiggot, had threatened England for impounding two of Howes's cows which England found on Sir John Hobart's land. When England was going home, Howes hit him with a stick.
337. See Robert Doughty of Aylsham to RD, 10 November 1665, Aylsham 304, explaining that Priest had many suits against him and had sold Allen two cows as part payment for fees due to Allen in executing a judgement. RD ordered Priest to pay Allen 10s. and have his animals returned to him.
338. Sir Thomas Rant's warrant, 8 November, Aylsham 347, for constables of Gimingham, Trunch, Bradfield and Southrepps to help Ellys search for his spade.
339. See R. Fisher to RD, 13 November 1665, Aylsham 193, requesting a warrant to 'ransack at large' for lost goods.
340. Warrant, Aylsham 1, orders John Miller and his wife also to appear.
341. 'Sir R. K.' is probably Sir Robert Kemp of Gissing, 2nd bart. (1627-1710).
342. See above 20 October 1665.
343. Undated information of both parties, Aylsham 347. Gedg, given

as a worsted weaver, denied lying with Everard (or Everett), who was his servant; she said Gedg had not promised to marry her.

344. Reverse foliation. The portion of the act's text which RD transcribed has not been reproduced here.

APPENDIX I:

Robert Doughty's Charges to Quarter Sessions Juries

Untitled charge, May-August 1662[1]

The due execution of the law is the life thereof, and for the yielding obedience to it and all process & proceeding of the same, every man at twelve years of age is as well to be sworn as for the bearing faith & true allegiance to the king's majesty, his heirs & lawful successors. And for the due execution of every ancient office in this kingdom (the kingly not excepted) & almost of every new, the law doth require from the officer one oath at least. Accordingly you whose several offices now are to inquire for your several hundreds, and you whose office is now to inquire at large for the body of this county, were now severally sworn due inquiry & true presentment to make of all such matters & things as should be given you in charge. Which, to make as short as I can (that the matter may not be lost in words), is that every of you in & by your several juries do, as is most proper or as here hath been most usual, respectively inquire & present all & every the offences, nuisances & annoyances and all & every the offender & offenders in every of them which are here inquirable & presentable.

And now although to those who have read the law & to you who by your frequent services here have grown perfect in them nothing need more to be added, yet because all of you may not be such & chiefly because charges (from the time they were delivered by indenture under seal) have been as well intended for the instruction of raw bystanders (to whom I confess myself fittest to speak) as for the direction of jurors, I shall run over the common heads (& for the help of weaker memories according to the common course) and only enlarge myself in some particulars, leaving the residue to those of able judgements & great abilities to be dilated in as they shall judge most suitable to the times & occasions.

All offences here inquirable & presentable are either immediately against God, the king or the subject, for in some respect or other they be all or almost all against all three. The offences immediately against God are conjuration & witchcraft {which are conspiracies with the devil against the only true God & are made with or after I know not what direful & execrable compacts, covenants, imprecations, oaths & vows}. The seeming difference between them is the conjurer seems to command the devil, the witch to entreat him {but in truth the devil leads them both captive at his will: II Timothy 2:26.}[2] Herein four offences in the offenders, their aiders, abettors & counselors are by the statute of 1 James c. 12 made felony without benefit of clergy. The first is the using, practising or exercising any innovation or conjuration of any evil & wicked spirit; the second the consulting, covenanting with, entertaining, employing, feeding or rewarding any evil and wicked spirit to or for any intent or purpose; the third the taking out of the grave or place where the dead body resteth, the dead body of any man, woman or child or any part thereof to be employed or used in any manner of witchcraft, sorcery, charm or enchantment; and the fourth the using, practising or exercising any witchcraft, enchantment, charm or sorcery whereby any person hath been killed, destroyed, wasted, consumed, pined or lamed in his or her body or any part thereof.

And so are the second offences in any of five other, whereof the first is the taking upon him or them by witchcraft, enchantment, charm or sorcery to tell or declare in what place any treasure of gold or silver should or might be found or had in the earth or other secret places; the second [is] the etc. [sic] where goods or things lost or stolen should be found or become; the third [is] the etc. to provoke any person to unlawful love; the fourth [is] the etc. to waste, destroy or impair any cattle or goods of any person, if done; and the fifth [is] the etc. to hurt or destroy any person in his or her body although the same be not effected & done. And the first offence in every of these five are punished in every offender by a year's imprisonment without bail or mainprise & by the offender's open standing once in every quarter of the year by the space of six hours upon the pillory in some market town on the market day or on the day of some fair to be kept there, and there openly confessing his or her error & offence.

Then you have conspiracy properly & strictly so called (which is committed by two or more indicting or appealing an innocent person falsely & maliciously of felony). The offenders herein duly indicted & convicted (which is everywhere throughout the charge intended where for haste 'tis not expressed) are to have that judgement the law terms villainous. That is to say, to be committed to prison, to have their wives & children thrown out of their houses, to have their houses & lands seized into the king's hands, their houses pulled down, their meadows ploughed up & their trees digged out, to forfeit their goods & chattels and to lose their freedom of the law forever. And though they be pardoned, they can never after be jurors or witness or bear any office of the grant of the king, queen or any nobles (it always hath in it willful & corrupt).

Perjury which is committed when any person in any judicial proceedings sweareth absolutely & falsely in a matter material to the issue or cause in question, of himself or by subornation of other. Subornation of perjury is committed by any who procureth another so to swear: 5 Elizabeth c. 9. The suborner forfeits £40 & if not worth so much is to be imprisoned without bail or mainprise for half a year & to stand upon the pillory an hour in the open market in the town where or next to the place where the offence was committed, & the perjured person forfeits £20 & must be imprisoned six months without bail or mainprise. And if he have not goods & chattels worth £20 he is to be set on the pillory in some market place in the county, city or borough where the offence was committed & there to have both his ears nailed, & both of them so long as the judgements are unreversed are disabled for testimony in any court of record.

Profane cursing & swearing [are] offences nowadays too frequent, for too many there are who in common & trivial speeches cannot forbear oaths & curses, whether they account them an ornament to their speech, security against their own known falsehoods or enforcements of belief, or that the custom therein make them insensible thereof: 21 James c. 20. Herein some are so foolishly wicked or horribly impious that they have inverted the old form of swearing, for whereas formerly men expressed the conditions of oaths & suppressed the imprecations, these express the imprecations only & that upon or against themselves, without mentioning or perhaps ever meaning the conditions. I am sure what fall short of swearing is horrid cursing. And every person for every time he or she swear or curse forfeit 12d. to the poor.

And whether hence I know not, another sort of men (commonly called Quakers) wholly deny to swear any manner of oath though by lawful authority thereunto duly required, as if to swear were absolutely evil & forbidden & would justify their opinion from the 5th chapter of St. Matthew [verse] 34, which forbids swearing in ordinary communication or by other than God, & from 5 St. James verse 12 where the apostle, commending the suffering of affliction & patience, above all things forbids swearing, which in such case is an high degree, if not the height of, impatience & in the devil's words & sense a cursing of God to the face: Job 2:5,9.

Whereas the Lord himself in the 45th chapter of Isaiah at verse 23 saith, I have sworn by myself, the word is gone out of my mouth in righteousness & shall not return, That unto me every knee shall bow, every tongue shall swear; and frequently in the old testament is said to have sworn by his life, his holiness, his great name etc. And an angel in either testament swore by him that liveth forever, and good men in both & without reproof, as St. Paul [in] Galatians 1:20, Behold before God I lie not; and [in] II Corinthians 1:18, But as God is true, and in Deuteronomy 6:13, the Israelites were commanded to swear by God's name. Indeed, they might not swear (neither may we) by any false god or creature or lightly or rashly or deceitfully or falsely. But that faith amongst them, & them & others, might be more firmly kept, they frequently used the promissory oath; and that truth in cases controverted might be the better discovered, they used the assertatory oath also. And so may we use both or either whensoever by lawful authority we shall be thereunto duly required. And in some cases we must under penalties, as twice refusing to take the oath of obedience subjects the refuser first to imprisonment without b[ail] or m[ainprise] and lastly to the pain & loss in a praemunire. And every witness served with process out of any court to testify his knowledge to whom a reasonable sum is tendered for his charges (unless he hath a sufficient let to the contrary) must accordingly appear or forfeiteth to the party grieved ten pounds & as much as he loseth for want of testimony of that witness: 5 Elizabeth c. 9.

And lately by parliament 'tis enacted that if any person or persons (who maintain that the taking of an oath in any case whatsoever, although before a lawful magistrate, is altogether unlawful & contrary to the word of God) from & after the 24th day of March 1662 shall willfully & obstinately refuse to take an oath, where by the law of the realm he or she is or shall be bound to take the same, being lawfully & duly tendered; or shall endeavour to persuade any other person to whom any such oath shall be in like manner duly & lawfully tendered to refuse & forbear the taking of the same; or shall by printing, writing or otherwise go about to maintain & defend that the taking of an oath in any case whatsoever is altogether unlawful; and if the persons commonly called Quakers shall at any time after the said 24th day of March depart from the places of their several habitations & assemble themselves to the number of five or more of the age of sixteen years or upwards at any one time in any place under pretence of joining in a religious worship not authorized by the laws of this realm; that the party in all and every such cases so offending[3] shall forfeit for the first offence such sum as shall be imposed not exceeding five pounds, & for the second offence such sum as shall be imposed not exceeding ten pounds (which forfeitures are to increase the stock of the house of correction & are) to be levied by warrant of the justices of oyer & terminer, of assize & gaol delivery, or of the peace, in any of their open sessions before whom the conviction shall be, by distress & sale of the offender's goods, rendering the overplus. And for want of such distress, or for nonpayment of the said forfeiture within one week after such conviction, the party so convicted shall be committed to the common gaol or house of correction for the first offence for three months & for the second offence for six months without bail or mainprise, there to be kept at hard labour; and for the third offence shall abjure the realm or otherwise the king may cause the offender to be transported in any ship to any of his majesty's plantations: 13 & 14 Charles II c. 2.

And this brings me to what concerns the worship of God, the places used for the same, the observation of the Lord's day, the abuses thereof & the unlawful pastimes used thereon. Our laws in times of popery have forbidden that any fair or market should be held or kept in any churchyard: 13 Edward I c. 6; or on any Good Friday or then principal feast or Sunday (the four in harvest excepted): 25 Henry VI c. 5. And after the reformation by 5 & 6 Edward VI c. 3 all Sundays & 27 other days in the year are commanded to be kept holy & bodily labour on them to be abstained & none other. But therein is provided that every husbandman, labourer, fisherman & other person & persons whatsoever upon the same holidays in harvest, or at any other time when necessity shall require, may labour, ride, fish or work any kind of work at their free wills & pleasures. And by the same parliament the malicious striker with any weapon or drawer of any weapon to strike in any church or churchyard is to have one of his ears cut off; or if he have no ears is to be branded on the cheek with an hot iron, having an 'F' thereon for a fighter or fraymaker & also to be ipso facto excommunicated: [5 & 6 Edward VI] c. 3.

Whosoever meet out of his, her or their parish for any sport or pastime whatsoever or use within the parish any unlawful exercises or pastimes (on the Lord's day) forfeit 3s. 4d. apiece [by] 1 Charles I c. 1 to the use of the poor. Carriers, waggoners, carmen, waymen and drovers travelling on the Lord's day with horse or horses, waggon or waggons, cart or carts, wain or wains or any[4] cattle, forfeit 20s. apiece [to the] poor: 3 Charles I c. 1. And butchers by themselves or other killing or selling any victual that day forfeit 6s. 8d. apiece. And shoemakers that shoe to sell & sell any boots, shoes, buskins, startups,[5] slippers or pantofles[6] on the Lord's day forfeit 3s. 4d. a pair & their value: 1 James c. 22. Saying, singing and hearing mass, the hearer forfeits 100 marks & is to suffer a year's imprisonment, & the sayer or singer thereof 200 marks & a year's imprisonment & thence till the 200 marks be paid: 23 Elizabeth c. 1. The parson, vicar, or other minister that ought to say the common prayer, refusing it or preaching,[7] declaring or speaking anything in the derogation or depraving of the same or anything therein contained, or that shall use any other order, form, matins or evening song etc. contrary to the statute of 1 Elizabeth c. 2 shall for his first offence lose a year profits of all his spiritual promotions & suffer six months' imprisonment without bail or mainprise, or if he have no such promotions 12 months' imprisonment as aforesaid, and further offending are to suffer such greater punishments as are mentioned in the said statute.

The declaring or speaking anything in the derogation, depraving or despising of the common prayer book or of anything therein contained; the interrupting or letting any parson, vicar or other minister to sing or say the common prayer book according to the said book; or the procuring any parson, vicar or other minister to say or sing the common prayer (or to administer the sacraments or either of them) otherwise than is mentioned in the said book, subjects each offender for the first offence to the forfeiture of an 100 marks, for the second of 400 marks & for the third to the forfeiture of all his or her goods & chattels and to imprisonment for life. Every person in the late queen's dominions having no lawful or reasonable excuse to the contrary should endeavour to resort to his or her parish church or chapel accustomed (or upon reasonable let thereof to some other) every Sunday & other holiday & then & there abide orderly & soberly during the common prayer, preachings or other service of God there to be used or be punished by the censure of the church & the forfeiture of 12d. to the use of the poor of the same parish by the churchwardens of the same by way of distress to be levied of the goods, lands & tenements of the offender. Now although this act of 1 Elizabeth c. 2 is by the new act of uniformity in suspense, yet on St. Bartholomew's Day next & thenceforth it will be of full force: 14 Charles II c. 2. As to the new common prayer book £3 per mensem.

And sodomy or buggery, which is a detestable violation of the order of our Almighty Creator and is said to be committed by man's carnal lying with man or by man's or woman's carnal lying with some beast and is felony without benefit of clergy: 25 Henry VIII c. 6 & 5 Elizabeth c. 17.

Those offences immediately against the king's majesty are high treason, some felonies, misprision of high treason and praemunires. High treason is committed, 25 Edward III c. 2, by encompassing or imagining the death of the king or of our lady his queen or of their eldest son & heir; by violating of her the king's companion or the king's eldest daughter unmarried or the wife of the king's eldest son & heir; by levying war against our lord the king in his realm, by adhering to in his realm, aiding or comforting anywhere his enemies, but every of these must be declared by open deed. By counterfeiting his great seal, privy seal, privy signet or sign manual: 1 Mary c. 6; by counterfeiting his money or any other current in England; by impairing or diminishing any of the said moneys for gain: 5 Elizabeth c. 11 & 18 Elizabeth c. 1; by bringing into England any counterfeit money, knowing it to be so, to merchandise therewith or to make payment thereof; by killing the chancellor or treasurer of England or any justice in his place doing his office; by having obtained or gotten since the last day of the first parliament of Queen Elizabeth any manner of bull, writing or instrument whatsoever from the bishop or see of Rome: 13 Elizabeth c. 2; by publishing or any way putting in use any such bull, writing or instrument; by Jesuits, popish or seminary priest or other ecclesiastical person howsoever called coming into being or remaining in the late queen's dominions contrary to the statute of 27 Elizabeth c. 2; by practising to absolve, persuade, or withdraw in any place within his majesty's dominions any of his majesty's English subjects from their natural obedience, or to reconcile them to the pope or see of Rome, or by moving them or any of them to promise obedience to any pretended authority to the see of Rome or other prince, state or potentate; by being therein willingly absolved or withdrawn as aforesaid or willingly reconciled, or by promising obedience to any such pretended authority, prince, state or potentate as aforesaid, except such reconciled person or persons within six days after his or their return into England (submit to his majesty & laws) before the bishop of the diocese or two justices of peace jointly or severally of the county where he shall arrive & take the oaths of supremacy & obedience: 3 James c. 4.

By refusing to take or not taking & pronouncing the oath of supremacy being the second time duly tendered (which must be three months after the first tender) and the refusal upon the first tender incurs a praemunire: 5 Elizabeth c. 1. By advised [sic], extolling or defending the authority, jurisdiction or power of the pope or see of Rome used or usurped in any the late queen's dominions or by wittingly attributing any such jurisdiction, authority or pre-eminence to either of them the second time, the offender in either case for the first offence incurs likewise a praemunire. And by compassing, imagining, inventing, devising or intending death or destruction or any bodily harm tending to death or destruction, maim or wounding, imprisonment or restraint of the person of the king's majesty that now is or to deprive or depose him from the style, honour or kingly name of the imperial crown of this realm or of any other his majesty's dominions or countries or to levy war against his majesty within this realm or without, or to move or stir any foreigner or strangers with force to invade this realm or any other his majesty's dominions or countries being under his obeisance: 14 Charles II, c. 2.

Whosoever hath committed any of these offences or contrived, counselled, commanded or aided any of them to be done, and whosoever hath received & comforted any who have done the same, knowing him, her or them to have so done (whose offence is neither misprision of high treason nor praemunire) are traitors: 13 Elizabeth c. 1 & 23 Elizabeth c. 1. But no person or persons shall be indicted or attainted of any offence now being or hereafter to be made high treason or petty treason unless accused by two lawful accusers (who if living at the time of the arraignment shall there avow what they have to say) unless the party or parties arraigned shall willingly without violence confess the same: 5 & 6 Edward VI c. 11. Two witnesses must accuse in treason, petty treason, misprision of treason & for the words: 1 Edward VI [c.] 12. And[8] two able and lawful witnesses who were by and present at the doing of the offence & according to law accused the offender or offenders for the same are sufficient & lawful witnesses.

The conspiring the death of the king's majesty, of any lord or other of the privy council or of the steward, treasurer or controller of the king's house, by any of the king's servants sworn & in his chequer roll, with any other, is felony: 3 Henry VII c. 14. Whosoever having the charge or custody of any the king's armour, ordnance, munition, shot, powder or habiliments of war, or of any victual provided for soldiers, gunners, mariners or pioneers[9] shall for lucre or gain advisedly & purposely to hinder his majesty's service at one or more times embezzle or convey away any of the same to the value of twenty shillings is a felon, but the impeachment must be within the year: 31 Elizabeth c. 4. Whosoever pass beyond sea to serve a foreign prince, state or potentate, or shall serve a foreign prince, state or potentate when he is beyond the sea & shall not have taken the oath of obedience is a felon: 3 James c. 4 & [blank]. Whosoever hath borne or shall bear any office in camp, army or company of soldiers or been conductor of soldiers and shall after go voluntarily to serve any prince, state or potentate before he hath entered bond with two sureties in £20 at least, conditioned that he shall not be reconciled to the pope or see of Rome nor enter into or consent to any practice, plot or conspiracy against the king, his heirs or successors or any of his dominions, but shall disclose to his said majesty, his heirs & successors or some lords of his or their privy council such practice, plot or conspiracy is a felon: 3 James c. 4, by this clause also.

The false forging or counterfeiting of any gold or silver not current in this realm is a misprision of high treason [by] 14 Elizabeth c. 3, & generally misprision of high treason is the knowing of any high treason & the keeping secret or concealing of the same: 1 Edward VI c. 12; 5 Edward VI c. 11; 13 Elizabeth c. 1; two witnesses [are required by] 1 Edward VI c. 12. Whereas every subject by his oath of allegiance is bound to make the same known (within 24 hours next after[10] any high treason comes to his knowledge) to some of his majesty's council or to some justice of peace. And let no man flatter himself with the secrecy of his treason or with impunity for the same, for God hath said, Curse not the king, no, not in thy thought, for a bird of the air shall carry the voice & that which hath wings shall tell the matter: Ecclesiastes 10:20.

And praemunires in which he or they by 27 Edward III c. 1 is or are that sue out of the realm for anything in the cognizance of the king's courts or of things whereof judgement is given in the king's courts or that sue in any other court (unless by attaint or error) to defeat or impeach any judgement given in the king's courts. And by 16 Richard II c. 5 [they] that purchase or sue or cause to be purchased or sued in the court of Rome or elsewhere any translations, processes, sentences of excommunications, bulls, instruments or any other things whatsoever which touch the king or be against him, his crown & his regality or realm, and the bringers, receivers, publishers & executors whatsoever, & their notaries, procurators, attorneys, counselors, maintainers, abettors & fautors[11] duly attainted (with him or them) shall be put out of the king's protection & forfeit their lands, goods & chattels to the king & have imprisonment of their bodies & be ransomed at the king's will & by the said 16 Richard II c. 5 they forfeit their tenements also. And before the statute of 5 Elizabeth c. 1 any man might have killed or slain them as well as a wolf or enemy of the king & his realm: 25 Edward III c. 22.

He or they that wittingly & willingly yield, give or contribute any money or other relief to or for any Jesuit, seminary or other priest, deacon or such other religious or ecclesiastical person or any college of Jesuits or seminary or any person then being of or in such college or seminary directly or indirectly or by any way or means is or are in the worst praemunire, which is of the said 16 Richard[12] II c. 5. 27 Elizabeth c. 2. And so is, are or shall be any person or persons that[13] since the 24th day of June 1661 hath or have or hereafter shall have maliciously & advisedly by writing, printing, preaching or other speaking expressed, uttered, declared or affirmed that the parliament begun at Westminster upon the 3rd day of November 1640 (known to you perhaps better by the name of the Long Parliament) is not yet dissolved or is not determined or that it ought to be in being or hath yet any continuance or existence or that there lies any obligation upon him or any other person from any oath, covenant or engagement whatsoever to endeavour a change of government, either in church or state or that both houses of parliament or either of them have or hath a legislative power without the king or any other words to the same effect: 13/14 Charles II c. 2.

And those offences immediately against the subject are petty treason, diverse felonies & other trespasses,[14] but on all these I cannot so largely insist as I have on the former. Petty treason is committed when one who oweth faith & obedience killeth the person to whom the same are owing, as a wife killing her husband, a servant his or her master or mistress, or a priest his prelate. A man herein offending is to be drawn & hanged & a woman to be drawn and burned, which is also a woman's express judgement in high treason, but a man's is to be drawn, hanged & quartered: 25 Edward III, c. 2.

Murder, which is the killing or poisoning of a man, woman or child with malice forethought or malice by law supplied, as where a magistrate or officer or any in aid of either of them is or are killed, where a robber kills a true man or a gaoler his prisoner by duress, or where any kills or poisons one for another, or where death ensues upon an unlawful act. Every offender herein is a felon & hath no benefit of clergy. He who thrusts or stabs another so as he dieth thereof within six months, who at the time of the[15] stab or thrust had not first struck or had a weapon drawn, is a felon & hath no benefit of clergy: 1 James c. 8. Every woman that hath been delivered of any bastard issue & endeavoureth by herself or others by drowning, secret burying thereof or otherwise so to conceal the death thereof, as it may not come to light whether it were born alive or not but be concealed, shall suffer death as in case of murder (except she can prove by one witness at least that it was born dead): 21 James c. 27.

Manslaughter is the willful killing of another without any malice forethought or by law supplied & is felony. Se defendendo is when one hath first retreated or is driven to a strait & then in his necessary defence kills his pursuer or assailer. This was murder before the Statute of Gloucester, 6 Edward I c. 9, & since is of course pardoned, but the offender's goods are yet forfeited. Chance medley is when one in an act otherwise lawful casually kills another. This was also murder before the Statute of Markbridge, 52 Henry III c. 26 & since the said Statute of Gloucester is also pardoned, but the offender's goods are yet forfeited, though neither be felony. I might tell you here of homicide dispunishable, 24 Henry VIII c. 5, & of homicide justifiable, but because they be not matters of your inquiry & some might take occasion thereby to satisfy their private malice or revenge under pretence of necessity & their own safety, I shall pass them, giving for caution the words of Solomon, A man that doth violence to the blood of any person shall fly to the pit: Let no man slay him: Proverbs 28:17.

Putting out the eyes or cutting out the tongue of any person of malice forethought is felony: 5 Henry IV c. 5. Rape, which is an unlawful carnal knowledge of a woman above ten years of age (so far as it may be had) against her will, 3 Edward I c. 13, or of one under that age with or against her will, 18 Elizabeth c. 7, is felony without etc. clergy. The taking any maid, widow or wife against her will, having goods or land or being an heir apparent, & marrying her to any of the misdoers or any other by their assent or defiling her and the procuring & abetting the same and also wittingly receiving the woman, are felonies without clergy: 3 Henry VII c. 12 & 39 Elizabeth c. 9.

Robbery is the open assaulting, affrighting & taking from any person any money or goods whatsoever & is felony. If the robbery be in or near an highway, it is felony without benefit of clergy: 1 Edward VI, c. 12. The cutpurse taketh from a person privily & without his knowledge, yet if that he taketh be above 12d. in value it is felony without benefit of clergy; if but of or under that value it is but petty larceny: 8 Elizabeth c. 4. Burglary is the breaking & entering in the night the mansion house of another with intent to kill any person therein or to commit some other felony there & is felony without benefit of clergy: 18 Elizabeth c. 7. Felonious taking of any goods out of any parish church or other church or chapel is felony without clergy: 1 Edward VI c. 12. Felonious breaking any house in the day or night, any person being therein & put in fear thereby, is also felony without benefit of clergy: 1 Edward VI c. 12.

The robbing in any part or parcel of any dwelling house or dwelling place, the owner or dweller, his wife, children or servants then being within the said house or place or in any other place within the precincts of the said house or place, sleeping or waking, is felony without clergy: 5 & 6 Edward VI, c. 9. The robbing in any booth or tent in any fair or market, the owner, his wife, children or any servant[16] then being within the same is felony without etc.: eodem. The felonious taking away in the daytime any money or goods to the value of 5s. or upwards out of any dwelling house or houses or any part thereof, or any outhouse or outhouses belonging to or used with any dwelling house or houses, although no person be then in the said house or outhouses, is felony without benefit of clergy: 39 Elizabeth c. 15. The willful burning of any dwelling house or barn wherein then was any corn or grain is felony without benefit of clergy: Poulter's case.

Grand larceny is the felonious taking, stealing and carrying away the personal goods of another above the value of 12d. (being none of the former offences) & is felony, and only the stealer of horse, gelding or mare & his accessories are without benefit of clergy. Petty larceny is when the goods stolen be but of the value of 12d. or under. The offender forfeit his goods if he flieth etc. & is to be whipped or otherwise corporally punished.

Breach of prison is when one in the stocks or gaol for treason or felony or suspicion of either of them by himself or other breaketh the prison & flieth away. If the offender was committed for treason, the offence is treason, if for felony, felony: 1 Edward II [sic]. And so it is in rescous, which is the felonious breaking or taking away of one under arrest for treason or felony or suspicion of either of them. And so also it is in every voluntary escape, which is when one that hath another under arrest or a prisoner in custody for treason or felony or suspicion of either of them suffers him to go where he list or at large. The keeper or underkeeper of a prison by duress enforcing his prisoner against his will to become an appellor is a felon.

Outlandish people calling themselves Egyptians, using no trade or merchandises (but going up & down deceiving the people) being 8 years old, continuing & remaining a month together in England & Wales or either of them are felons without benefit of clergy: 1 & 2 Philip & Mary c. 4. And all born within the late queen's dominions that shall be seen or found in the company or fellowship of any commonly calling themselves or called Egyptians or that in their speech, apparel or behaviour shall counterfeit such for a month at one or several times are also felons without benefit of clergy: 5 Elizabeth c. 20.

The willing embezzling any record or parcel thereof or writ, return, panel, process or warrant of attorney in the courts of chancery, either benches or exchequer or in the king's treasury, whereby any judgement shall be reversed, is felony: 8 Henry VI c. 12. And every person that shall acknowledge or procure to be acknowledged any fine or fines, recovery or recoveries, deed or deeds enrolled, statute or statutes, recognizance or recognizances, bail or bails, judgement or judgements in the name or names of any other person or persons not privy or consenting to the same is a felon without benefit of clergy, except every attorney of record for judgements: 21 James c. 26.

Forgery is committed by any who contrary to the statute of 5 Elizabeth c. 14 have falsely forged or made or subtly caused or assented to be forged or made any false deed, charter or writing sealed, court roll or will in writing, to the intent the freehold or inheritance or the right title or interest of any person or persons in any freehold or copyhold lands, tenements or hereditaments might or should be molested, charged or recovered or have pronounced, published or shown forth in evidence any such as true, knowing the same to have been false & forged. And every offender herein shall pay the party grieved double costs & damages, be set in the pillory & there have both his ears cut off & his nostrils slit & cut and seared with an hot iron & shall forfeit to the king the issues & the profits of his lands & tenements for his life & during the same suffer perpetual imprisonment.

Or if such forgery have been to the intent that any person or persons should or might have or claim any estate or interest for term of years of, in or to any lands, tenements or hereditaments (not being copyhold) or any annuity in fee simple, fee tail or for life, lives or years, or have forged, made or caused or assented to be forged or made as aforesaid, any obligation or bill obligatory or any acquittance, release or other discharge of any debt, account, action, suit, demand or other personal thing, or have pronounced, published or given in evidence any such as true, knowing the same to be false, every offender is to pay the party grieved his double costs & damages & be set in the pillory & there have one of his ears cut off & suffer imprisonment without bail or mainprise for one whole year. And if any person that have been convicted of any the said offences in forgery have committed any of them the second time, he is a felon without benefit of clergy: 5 Elizabeth c. 14. But this act doth not extend to any lawyer, attorney, proctor or advocate for pleading, showing forth or giving in evidence any such forgery or forgeries.

Who findeth a falcon or other long-winged hawk & doth not presently carry it to the sheriff of that county is a felon: 37 Edward III, c. 19. Hunters by night or with painted faces in any forest, park or warren, rescuing themselves or disobeying so as the warrant for their apprehension be not satisfied, or willfully concealing the hunting, or any person faulty with the person examined thereupon, are felons: 1 Henry VII c. 7 (otherwise but trespassers).

Confederacies of masons, any that cause chapters & congregations of masons to be yearly assembled & holden are felons, and all other masons that come thereunto are to be imprisoned & fined and ransomed at the king's will: 3 Henry VI c. 1.

Marrying another husband or wife, the former being living, is felony except 1) where the one have been continually for 7 years absent beyond sea, 2) or the one have lived 7 years from the other in the king's dominions & neither of them known the other in that time to be living, 3) or the ecclesiastical courts have declared the first marriage void or divorced the married parties before the time of the second marriage, 4) or where either of the first married parties was at that first marriage within age of consent: 1 James c. 11.

To use to multiply gold or silver, or to use the craft of multiplication is felony, not that any did it but because impostors inveigled & cheated covetous & credulous persons by pretending they could do it: 5 Henry IV c. 5.

The breaking up or cutting down powdike,[17] oldfield dike or any other bank of the rind[18] or utmost part of that country [by] 22 Henry VIII c. 11 & 2 & 3 Philip & Mary c. 19 is felony.

Papist or sectary that should abjure the realm & refuse, or that abjure & depart not accordingly, or that departing return without his majesty's special licence is a felon without benefit of clergy for any of these offences: 35 Elizabeth c. 1,2. Whosoever wittingly & willingly receive, relieve, comfort, aid or maintain any Jesuit, seminary priest or other priest, deacon or religious or ecclesiastical person born within the late queen's dominions [and] made, ordained or professed by any authority derived or pretended from the see of Rome & being at liberty, knowing him to be such, is a felon without benefit of clergy: 27 Elizabeth c. 2.

Whosoever being infected with the plague after commandment to keep house converseth abroad with company, if he hath a plague sore not cured is a felon, if he hath none is to be punished as a vagabond: 1 James c. 31. A banished rogue returning without lawful licence or warrant is a felon: 39 Elizabeth c. 4. A branded rogue begging or wandering again is a felon without benefit of clergy: 1 James c. 7.

Household servants of lords & others of good degree that take, spoil & distribute amongst them the goods of their dead lord & master & do not appear in the King's Bench at the day specified in the writ made & proclaimed according to the statute of 33 Henry VI c. 1 are felons. Every servant (not being an apprentice or under the age of 18 years) to whom his or her master or mistress deliver any caskets, jewels, money or other goods to keep, that withdraw him or herself from his or her said master or mistress & go away with the same or any part thereof with intent to steal the same or defraud his or her said master or mistress, embezzle the same or any part thereof or convert the same to his or her own use with purpose to steal it, if the same goods so gone away with or purposed to be stolen be of the value of 40s. or above it is felony: 21 Henry VIII c. 7 & 1 Elizabeth c. 10.

All who have brought, delivered, sent, received or taken or procured to be brought, delivered, sent or received into any ship or bottom any rams, sheep or lambs or any other kind of sheep to be carried or conveyed alive out of England, Wales, Ireland or any other the late queen's dominions, their aiders, abettors, procurers & comforters for the first offences forfeit all their goods, must be imprisoned for a year without bail & mainprise & then in the fullness of some market have their left hands cut off & nailed up in the openest place of such market. For their hands [they may have benefit of] clergy; and every of them then so offending again is a felon: 8 Elizabeth c. 3.

Every soldier, mariner or gunner that hath taken any prest or wages to serve the king on the sea, the land or beyond sea, departing the king's service without licence of his captain or the king's lieutenant there, is a felon without clergy: 7 Henry VII c. 1 & 3 Henry VIII c. 5; 20 Henry VI c. 19 & 5 Elizabeth c. 4. Every soldier serving the king in his wars in any of his dominions or on the seas or beyond the seas that being out of garrison depart the service without licence of his lieutenant or of the captain or warden, vice-admiral, high admiral or the king's deputy or lieutenant or in their absence by any of their deputies is a felon without benefit of clergy: 2 & 3 Edward VI c. 2. And here I desire you would take notice that every soldier that hath served as aforesaid is to return the harness & the horse, gelding or mare he was set out with to the owner, his executors or administrators, or upon his or their complaint & due proof thereof made any one justice of the peace where the soldier shall be found may commit him to ward, there to remain without bail or mainprise until satisfaction for the same be made to the party grieved. Except the soldier bring a sufficient testimony or warrant before the justice from the lieutenant or any the above-named persons under his hand & seal, testifying the horse or harness were lost in service against the soldier's will or taken from him by the said lieutenant or any of the above-named persons & appointed to some other, and then he is to be discharged thereof and the other soldier to be charged therewith as aforesaid. By knowing the law[19] and by close adhering to your right herein, you may henceforth by God's blessing prevent your beating with your own weapons and your soldiers and servants from becoming masters or lords over you.

All idle & wandering soldiers or mariners or idle persons wandering as soldiers or mariners are felons without benefit of clergy: 39 Elizabeth c. 17. And so is every idle & wandering soldier or mariner coming from his captain from or beyond the seas who shall not have a testimonial under the hand of some one justice of peace of or near the place where he landed, setting down the time & place where he landed & the place of his dwelling or birth to which he is to pass & a convenient time for his passage limited therein; or who shall have such testimonial & shall willingly exceed the time therein limited above fourteen days (except he fall sick by the way, & then he is to settle himself in some lawful course of life or within convenient time to pass according to his testimonial). And so also is every idle & wandering soldier or mariner or other person wandering as soldier or mariner, who have counterfeited or forged any such testimonial or have with him any such counterfeit or forged testimonial knowing it to be such. And every of these idle & wandering felons are according to their judgements to be executed, except some honest freeholder to be allowed by the justice before whom the felon or felons shall be arraigned, or some person valued at the last subsidy at £10 in goods or £10 in lands, will take him or them into his service for one whole year then next following and be then bound in a recognizance in £10 to keep him or them for one whole year & bring him or them to the next sessions of the peace & gaol delivery after the said year. And every person so retained departing within such year without licence of such master is to be tried again as a felon & to have no benefit of clergy: 39 Elizabeth c. 17. But this law is not to extend to any poor soldier or mariner coming from or beyond the seas who is by a justice of peace licensed in convenient time to pass the next & direct way to the place to which he is to repair, although he ask and take relief in his travel.

Transporting or carrying out of the realm silver in money or otherwise (except the silver vessels great men when they go out of the realm have to serve in their houses) is felony. Searchers at ports & elsewhere for their encouragement are to have one-third part of such money as they find on the sea passing out of the realm, and in case they be found negligent or disobedient in searching, their bodies, lands, tenements, goods & chattels are to be taken & seized into the king's hand until they have made fine. But if they willingly suffer such silver or money to be transported, they also are felons: 17 Edward III not printed. And the carrying of any wool (which pass not the Straits of Marrock) or woolfells out of this realm (contrary to the statute of 18 Henry VI c. 15) is felony (to other places than the staple of Calais without the king's licence).

In petty treason, murder and other felonies, all that be any way guilty and present when the offence is committed are principals. But in all and every of them there be or may be accessories before & after the fact or felony committed.[20] Accessories before the fact are they who have contrived, aided, counselled, commanded, hired or procured the felony to be done. Accessories after the fact are they that know the principal have done the felony and notwithstanding receive and comfort him. The accessory is to suffer as his principal, but if the principal be not for the same felony attainted by outlawry or judgement (to be hanged by the neck till dead) the accessory is to be acquitted. And every offender in felony or any greater offence upon judgement must plead generally guilty or not guilty, or especially, as autrefois acquit, [autrefois] convict[21] or attaint etc. as the case shall be, but cannot plead any justification, for such offences are not justifiable. But it is contrary in trespass, for there the offender must plead his justification & rely upon it (till it be overruled by the court) or otherwise he shall have no benefit of it though his jury shall especially find it: St. 15 [sic]; 8 Elizabeth c. 4; 18 Elizabeth c. 7.

And this brings me to trespasses, which are of themselves sufficient for an whole charge, for in or about them are or may be more offences committed than I have already enumerated. And to speak my thoughts freely, to have made these the chief subject of this charge had been most suitable to your present service, and I had sometime a resolution so to have done, but when I had gathered together the particulars & began to consider & digest them, I found that the practice in many (& those no mean matters) ran contrary to the rule of law & that the law in diverse cases was not clear & that authority (or opinions rather) in such points were inconsiderable few or none. And thereupon I left the same as a fitter subject for some able person & for the consideration of parliament if it might be in the meantime, being loath preposterously[22] to begin at the wrong end or inconsiderably to encounter such difficulties with my weak & single abilities. And therefore now (for the help of your memories) I shall only name them to you, and so leave you to your inquiries into all offences touching or concerning every of them & then as briefly conclude.

They be hues & cries: 13 Edward I c. 1; misprision of felony, theftboot, getters of money or other things by false letters or tokens: 33 Henry VIII c. 1; going or riding armed: 2 Edward III c. 3, especially any of the late disbanded armies; affrays or any things done in terror of the people, menaces, assaults, batteries, blooddraughts (specially in the king's court or courts of record), mayhems, riots, routs, unlawful assemblies, forcible entries & detainers, 5 Richard [number illegible] c. 7, 8 Henry VI c. 9. Common barrators:[23] 34 Edward III c. 1[?]; maintenance:[24] 58 Edward III c. 17, 37 Henry VIII c. 7; champerty:[25] 33 Edward I; embracery:[26] 34 Edward III c. 8; & jurors taking to give their verdict: 38 Edward III c. 12. Exaction & extortion in sheriffs, in coroners: 3 Henry VII c. 1; in ordinaries about wills or administrations etc.: 21 Henry VIII c. 5; and in ministers for mortuaries or corpses present, [21 Henry VIII]

c. 5; & all other contempts, frauds, deceits & oppressions. Games.

The annoyances in & decays of highways & defaults in parishioners not coming six days & working for the amending the same: 2 & 3 Philip & Mary; 5 Elizabeth c. 13 etc. Nuisances in casting of dung, filth, entrails or garbages into any ditch, river or place to the infecting the air or prejudicing the healths of the inhabitants: 12 Richard II c. 13; or stopping up of windows, ways, gutters, drains, sewers etc. All destruction of the game & all unlawful use thereof. Putting by or encroaching upon ways, passages & paths, especially to the church, mill & market. Forestallers, engrossers, regrators: 5 Edward VI c. 14; 13 Elizabeth c. 25; 5 Elizabeth c. 12; unlawful weights & measures: 7 Henry VII c. 4 & 11 Henry VII, c. 1. Goldsmiths: 8 Henry V c. 3; pewterers, brasiers: 19 Henry VII c. 6, 4 Henry VIII c. 7; bakers, brewers, butchers, fishmongers, coopers, millers, maltsters, tanners, curriers, shoemakers, tilemakers: 17 Edward IV c. 4; clothiers, spinsters. Conspiracies of tradesmen, artificers & labourers to sell victual or to work at certain rates or prices etc. or not to end what other have begun & left: 2 Edward VI c. 15; or taking work & leaving the same unfinished contrary to agreement & the law: 5 Elizabeth c. 4. Undertaking apprentices & servants, masters, mistresses & dames as to service, departing or putting out of service or giving or taking excessive wages: 5 Elizabeth c. 4.

Taverners, innkeepers, alehousekeepers & victualers not observing the law & their articles and all recognizances entered by them or any of them with their sureties or by any other & forfeited. Tipplers, drunkards, keepers of gaming houses & gamesters therein & all other playing at unlawful games. Procurers, contrivers & publishers of libels or fond fantastical or false prophecies: 5 Elizabeth [sic]. Cottages new erected or newly converted & since continued: 43 Elizabeth c. 2. Unlicensed alehouses & such as lodge strangers in upland towns they will not answer for. Then incorrigible rogues and vagabonds: 39 Elizabeth c. 4 & 1 James c. 7. And lastly Winchester watch, which should by securing them secure us against them: 8 October 13 Edward I [sic].

But I will no longer detain you from your work. These things I have said that you might learn and remember it, and my exhortation to you is that you would perform and do it. And my close to all, as well upon the bench as at the bar, shall be the precept of our Saviour, Judge not according to the appearance, but judge righteous judgement: John 7:24.

[Notes appended to the text]

[Notes on 31 Henry VIII c. 14 requiring witnesses to appear and give evidence at trials of putative criminal offenders]

[Notes on the new act for highways]

[Excerpt from a statute prohibiting the export of sheep and wool to Scotland or any foreign part]

[Text of the oath of allegiance]

[Text of the oath of supremacy]

['An admonition to simple men deceived by malicious,' explaining the nature of Queen Elizabeth's title]

[Text of the oath of obedience]
[Text of the oath of the justices made 18 Edward III]
[Text of the oath of a justice of peace]
[Text of 'a dedimus, the label and return thereof & of the oaths of supremacy & justice of peace annexed thereto']
[Text of the grand jury's oaths]
[Text of the petty jury's oath]
[Notes on the act of uniformity]

'A charge provided to be spoken to the goodmen at Walsingham 15 October Anno Domini 1663'[27]

Gentlemen: When justice seats were held in the same counties but once in seven years (which was long before the invention of printing), the way then to inform the people in the law was by solemn charges given at such justice seats, which in those times were held & continued for forty days together (unless their works were in less time dispatched) and that in one place. And then the jurors for each hundred had their charge first read to them and after delivered them in writing (indented interchangeably under the hands & seals of the justices in eyre, and of the four knights for each hundred), who upon their oaths returned the jurors for their own hundred, which jurors returned their particular answer in writing to every chapter or article of the same (though they were in number near about seven score).

But as that course was found inconvenient so by degrees the same was here altered & brought to the order now used, where we have six justice seats in one year, the two assizes and the four general quarter sessions, and for the ease of the inhabitants of this county, each & every of the same sessions are held at three times on several days & at several places certain & foreknown. And this sessions is now according to the usual course here held by adjournment for these parts and is begun & to be ended this day. So as now, what by printing the law & most of it in the English tongue, by charges frequently given both at assizes & sessions, and by the experience you or most of you have heretofore had & gained in this service, you so well understand your duty in the same that now to give you a long charge may neither be necessary nor (respecting the time) convenient, this day being (short &) now far spent & too much of it lost by occasion of some men's late coming here.

And therefore now to waste no more words or time, as you who are now to inquire at large for the body of this county have even now expressly or impliedly sworn diligent inquiry & true presentment to make of all such matters & things as shall be given you in charge, so I do hereby charge you & every of you in & by this inquest accordingly to inquire and present all high treasons, misprisions of high treason, petty treasons, murders, manslaughters, witchcrafts, buggeries, rapes, robberies, burglaries, burning any dwelling house or houses or barn or barns with corn, grand larcenies, petty larcenies & other felonies whatsoever. Praemunires, misprisions of felony, theftboots, negligent escapes, getters of money or other things by false letters or tokens, refusing or dissuading any to take any lawful oath when duly tendered or maintaining that the taking of an oath in any case whatsoever is altogether unlawful; profane cursing & swearing, perjuries, conspiracies, forgeries. All going or riding armed (especially any of the late disbanded armies), affrays or anything done in terror of the people, menaces, assaults (especially such assault or affray as any servant, workman or labourer hath willfully made upon master, mistress, dame or any other that then had the charge or oversight of the work or of such in the work), batteries, blooddraughts (especially in any the king's courts or in any court of record), mayhems. Striking or drawing any weapon to strike in any church or churchyard, the keeping any fair or market in the latter of them, the disturbing on purpose any licensed preacher in his open sermon in either of them, the rescuing any such disturber being apprehended, the parish where any such disturbance hath been made that hath suffered such disturber to escape unapprehended. Quakers to the number of five or more of sixteen years of age or upwards that have assembled together at any time since the 24th day of March 1662 in one place, being none of their habitation, under pretence of joining in a religious worship. Riots, routs, unlawful assemblies, forcible entries & detainers, common barratries, maintenances, champerties, embraceries, jurors taking to give their verdict. Exactions, extortions especially in sheriffs, in coroners, in ordinaries about wills or administrations or in ministers for mortuaries or corpses present. All annoyances in & decays of bridges & highways, all nuisances & other annoyances.[28]

Forestallers, engrossers, regrators; unlawful balances, weights & measures; goldsmiths, pewterers, brasiers, bakers, brewers, coopers, butchers, fishmongers, millers, maltsters, tanners, curriers, shoemakers, tilemakers, clothiers & spinsters failing in their respective duties in or about their several occupations. Conspiracies of tradesmen, artificers or labourers to sell victual or to work at certain rates or prices or to work but at certain hours & times or to do but so much in a day, or not to end work other have begun and left, or taking work & leaving the same unfinished; refusing to take apprentices and undue taking of them; servants, masters, mistresses & dames, as to undue retaining into, departing or putting out of service or giving or taking of excessive wages.

Taverners, innkeepers, alehousekeepers & victualers not observing the law or their articles, and all recognizances entered by them or any of them with their sureties or by any other and forfeited. Tipplers, drunkards, keepers of gaming houses and gamesters playing therein, and all other playing at unlawful games, sports & exercises used on the Lord's day, and all other profanations thereof by waggoners, carmen, carriers, drovers, butchers and shoemakers. Sayers or singers & hearers of mass; procurers, contrivers & publishers of libels or fond fantastical & false prophecies.

Cottages at any time since & contrary to the statute of 31 Elizabeth c. 7 erected or converted & for every month or more continued, and inmates or more families than one placed or willingly suffered for every month or more in any cottage (contrary to the law). Unlicensed alehouses and such as lodge strangers in upland towns they will not answer for; rogues &

vagabonds; the not keeping of Winchester watch and the not following of hues & cries. All contempts in transgressing any statute whereof this court hath cognizance (especially if penned in the negative) or in not due performing or executing process, warrants & lawful commands of any justice or justices of the peace. Undersheriffs, bailiffs, stewards (as well of leets as turns), constables, gaolers, governors of bridewells & other officers who have presumed to misbehave themselves in their offices or have been in the same lukewarm, slack or negligent. All destruction of gentlemen's game and all unlawful use thereof; the keeping of unlawful guns and the unlawful shooting in any such or in any other [sic]. And all other contempts, forces, frauds, deceits and oppressions, and all & every other trespass & trespasses and offence & offences whatsoever, and all and every the offender & offenders whosoever in & about them & every or any of them throughout this charge mentioned, who and which are here by law and of right inquirable & presentable.

Which that you may now the better do you are seriously to consider your duty in this service to which you have been called and even now by solemn oath charged. Which ordinarily you do perform either upon the testimony of witness upon oath or upon the knowledge of you or some or one of you (every one's knowledge declared to his fellow jurors being to be by them admitted as the testimony of such a witness) or else upon both. And in which you all (who are therein neither to regard rich or poor, friend or foe (as such) but the truth and merit of the case) are to proceed with great exactness & strictness, being the eyes of this court for the impartial discovering of all such offences & of the offenders in the same, that they may be according to the law charged with and upon lawful convictions be duly punished for the same. Which unless you first perform on your parts we cannot do on ours; but upon your performance (I hope I may clearly declare that) on our parts we will not be wanting.

And herein I shall only give you the direction and caution mentioned in your oath, that you present nothing for hatred, malice or evil will, fear, favour, reward or hope of reward, for herein you are not to remember any private[29] grudges or return or requite[30] former injuries, much less take vengeance[31] with despiteful heart for old hatred. You are not to afflict the just or take a bribe, for a gift doth blind the eyes of the wise & pervert the matters of the righteous. Neither are you to favour any vice for the person's sake or hate any person for his vice, nor in judgement respect persons but hear the small as well as the great and not be afraid of the face of man, for the judgement is God's.

And so I shall conclude with this brief exhortation, that as you have sworn in the presence and name of God (who is a discerner of the thoughts and intents of the heart) diligently & truly to inquire and present such matters & things as you now have in charge, so that in his name & fear, as well for the due & full observance of your oaths as for the satisfaction & preservation of the king's laws and peace, the defence & safeguards of the subjects' persons and estates, and the discouragement and punishment of offenders & offences (considerations to be ever highly esteemed by all just and honest men), you would now do the same faithfully and with a perfect heart.

Ezekiel 25:15, 35:5-11; Amos 5:12; Deuteronomy 16:19, 1:17 Hebrews 4:12; II Chronicles 19:9.

'A charge provided to be spoken at Fakenham 4 August 1664, being my third charge in course'[32]

My lords and gentlemen and more particularly you who shall here this day serve in any jury and most especially you who are already sworn on this grand inquest:

The Lord said (as you may find in the 18th chapter & 20th verse of Genesis) because the cry of Sodom & Gomorrah is great, and because their sin is very grievous, I will go down now and see whether they have done altogether according to the cry of it, which is come unto[33] me; and if not I will know. And this our eternal God did not say in regard of himself, for he and he only[34] ever was and forever shall be both omnipresent and omniscient. But this he did & left for & as a precedent of justice & judgement unto men, and imparted the same unto (faithful) Abraham who was to become a great & mighty nation, and in whom all the nations on the earth were to be blessed, knowing that he would command his children & household after him, and that they should keep the way of the Lord, to do justice & judgement as 'tis said in the context there.

According unto which precedent (in capital & other criminal offences) is the common law of this our English nation framed & practised. Where by it such excellent provisions are made, & by its judges so great cares are taken that the truth may be fairly & fully found out & discovered, that the innocent & oppressed may be freed & acquitted and that only the guilty may be condemned & punished (and such punishments are also executed with so much mercy) that the whole world hath not the like elsewhere. For here no secret informations are made, no private inquisitions are taken, no loose & flying reports are credited, no uncertain & wandering fames are pressed against, no enforced confessions are extorted from, nor any kind of tortures are used to any offender or offenders whosoever.

Neither is any such offender (unless in cases of peerage) at this day concluded guilty, convicted or attainted of or for any such offence (if by the law he will justify himself) but by presentment & verdict upon oath of four & twenty men at the least (being two full juries & men) of good estates & honest condition. And in case of peerage but by such presentment of 12 such men or more upon oath and the verdict of twelve[35] peers or more upon their allegiance. Which in both cases are to be made and given in the face of justice in the proper open courts upon their or some of their knowledges and the testimony of credible & sufficient witness upon oath, or upon either of them, where the witnesses, offender & triers (whether peers or jury) are all face to face. And the witnesses openly give their testimony and the offender have free liberty to answer for himself, to interrogate those witnesses (if not immediately by himself, mediately by the court) for clearing their evidence & more fully discovering the truth, and to produce his own witnesses to testify anything material on his behalf.

And the verdict of such triers thereupon given is taken for to be the very truth.

Nor, though if after his offence committed he doth so withdraw himself that (upon such legal process as are made for his apprehension) he cannot be taken in the county where the same was committed; or if after his offence he flieth for the same and be taken; or if upon his arraignment for the same he of malice standeth mute or will not directly answer, or challengeth of the jury returned for or in order to his trial without just cause by himself showed & by the court allowed, in high treason above thirty-five or in petty treason, murder or other felony above twenty [prospective jurors] (every of which the law looks upon even as a tacit or implied confession thereof); or if upon his examination by or before any justice of the peace he expressly confesseth the offence and after upon his arraignment denieth it; doth the common law (lest the offender might be enforced or otherwise induced thereunto by the threats, promises, terrors or frauds of other, or by his own ignorance of the law, or too great fear & lest any innocent should suffer) in any of these cases or in any other conclude the offender guilty of his offence until he hath been presented or indicted for the same by twelve such men or more, and until by his lawful triers (whether peers or jury) he be convicted of the same or of his contumacious refusal to justify himself by the law, of which the court by their own view or hearing is not fully satisfied, except in the first case where if he be not taken or he yieldeth not himself before the return of the exigent he is attainted by outlawry.

Nor if upon his arraignment for the same (though he doth confess it, which if recorded is an attainder of itself and the fullest for the satisfaction of the judge) doth the judge (who in all ordinary matters in capital offences is the offender's only counsel), if he perceive the confession do proceed from fear, menace or duress, record the same against him, but advise him to put himself upon his trial by his country, who are ordinarily twelve of the twenty-four who are or should be of the most substantial people & worthy credit & not suspect (of partiality), living nearest & having best knowledge of the fact, returned or impanelled for such trials by the sheriff without procurement. And herein the offender may take his lawful exceptions, either to the whole array or panel or to any[36] of the polls or persons therein, or of the tales[37] (or such other like men) as shall be added thereto as they come to be sworn, for any lawful cause showed & allowed, as partiality, want of hundred or 40s. freehold per annum. Yea and besides these challenges for cause, wherein he is not limited to any number, the law allows him in favour of his life to challenge of them peremptorily or without any cause showed or allowed any number in petty treason, murder or other felony not exceeding twenty and in high treason (in every case where peremptory challenge is not by statute taken away) not exceeding five & thirty.

And as this fully declared the most excellent and extraordinary fair frame and practice of our common law, so thence I cannot forbear to commend unto you (though I cannot sufficiently extol) the free & happy estate & condition of every free-born English subject, who here loseth neither limb, life, lands or goods, without his own fact or default. Nor then until after such legal presentment of his offence (whether the same be felonious or more heinous) as I have already mentioned, he appears upon record to have withdrawn himself or made a flight in law for the same, that is to say, so to have absented himself without reasonable cause (as imprisonment or being beyond sea) that he could not be found and came not in upon such process as were made for his apprehension for the same, before the alias capias or second capias[38] was returned and the exigent[39] was thereupon awarded against him; or be convicted thereof by his own free confession upon his arraignment or by his standing mute or not direct answering in high treason or by his peremptorily challenging above 35 in high treason or above 20 in felony, or by the verdict of his triers (whether peers or jury) as before I have said, by which he loseth his goods, and thereupon is attainted by outlawry or judgement, whereby he loseth limb, life & lands, or any of them, except where the person be acquitted of the felony or treason and be found by that or any other jury or[40] coroner's inquest to have made a flight in fact or actually to have fled for the same, who thereby loseth his goods. And also except such felonious or murderous offender as refuseth to justify himself by the law and at his arraignment standeth mute of malice or will not directly answer, who thereupon hath his judgement to be put to his penance or to be pressed to death & thereby forfeiteth his goods. And his goods are also forfeited who is found by any coroner's inquest or jury to have killed himself feloniously or to have been a felon & to have fled for the same, and to have been necessarily killed in the pursuit or to have killed some other by chancemedly[41] or in his own defence.

And now lest any[42] should think that the common law by such high care lest any innocent should suffer, and by providing such solemn trials for offenders, hath thereby encouraged them & given them hopes to get through or escape with lenity or impunity, I shall proceed & show you how the common law hath also provided such choice means for their prevention and such strict ways for their discoveries that we may justly wonder why any should be & how any should be concealed or escape.

First, everyone in the oath of allegiance (which he either hath taken or is supposed to have taken) hath or ought to have sworn that he will commit no felony or treason or consent to either. And next all persons throughout this kingdom were put into tithings and every tithingman engaged that himself & his whole tithing should keep the peace & be forthcoming upon any call or lawful demand. And he that none would so engage for was to be kept in the gaol. Besides, no persons were or are to be permitted to live idly, and poor persons had and are yet to have competent relief. And those honest ages (wherein these things were strictly observed) had no insurrections or rebellions and few felons. Yet for their apprehensions upon every felony committed, quick & fresh suit was (& yet is) to be made, hue & cry to be levied & by all men pursued from town to town & from country to country, as well by horsemen as footmen. And no doubt but as they went they searched fully & thoroughly all places suspected to harbour the felon or to have the stolen goods (for it could be to no purpose to run the hue & cry into other countries when the felon & goods were at home). And all rogues, such as ran on messages for thieves, such as slept on the day & watched on the night, & such as frequented alehouses & fared well & had no visible means of livelihood, were & yet are to be examined. And the felons, or those found suspected for the felony, being taken were to be delivered to the sheriff of the county where so taken, as since & yet they are to be brought before some justice of the peace to be examined & disposed of in order to their trials. And all men who made default in such hue & cry (or shall so do) were & are to be grievously fined, and if lords to lose their franchises, if bailiffs to have a year's imprisonment & to be grievously fined, & if they had not to pay such fine to be two years imprisoned. And every sheriff, coroner or bailiff for favour concealing such felony or not attaching such felon or not doing their office against such, was & yet is to be grievously fined at the king's pleasure, and not having to satisfy such fine was & is to have three years imprisonment.

But this way being exceeding troublesome and the thief being commonly a lurking rogue & at home, the party grieved went & yet goeth to some justice of peace for his warrant directed to the constables of the place to search there for such felon & goods. Which hath done the work with far less noise, charge & trouble and yet in ordinary cases with as much or more certainty, being a private hue & cry, managed at the least by one known & sworn officer of his majesty's within his own command in the presence of the party grieved, who might be best presumed to know his own. Yet sometimes this way hath been held scarce lawful and by some to have some inconveniences. But by two acts, one of the last & the other of this session of the parliament now adjourned, its legality is cleared. For by the first, power is given to one justice of peace to do so in diverse cases which be not felony, and by the last, two or more of the officers of the king's navy are empowered to grant such warrant for inquiry & search, for any of the store or ammunition of the king's shipping or navy embezzled or filched away, as justices of peace may do in case of felony. And the inconveniences or rather particular mischiefs may be prevented by granting such warrants to none but discreet & honest persons, or by limiting them to the persons by name or to such as dwell in such a town or place therein, or by requiring the return of each within a short time and withal an account of what hath been done thereupon, for I do think that under such restrictions scarce any will dare to do unhandsome things.

And now as I have showed you what courses were taken to prevent offences before done and to discover the offenders when done, so now I am come to show you the several times, places and ways of their prosecutions for such doings, wherein I will not meddle with the trial by ordeal or any other taken away but only those three which have been & yet are or may be used.

The first was a trial by the manor (and this I mention first because it was first disused), and the last case I have read of was this. A robber upon the highway upon fresh suit was apprehended & brought in at an assizes. The judge only examined the party robbed, where, by whom & of what he was robbed (which was of a mail[43] or portmantle in which were diverse goods) of which after the person robbed had given a full account, the judge caused the mail to be opened[44] in court, and seeing that the account was true forthwith gave the mail & goods to their owner & judgement of death upon the robber, who was executed accordingly. And in court barons having the liberty of infangthief & outfangthief, such thieves upon proof by the witnesses of the person robbed or from whom the goods were stolen that the goods were that person's were, without being put to answer for the same, adjudged to death & after executed (now an infangthief is a tenant or other person living within such manor and apprehended therein upon fresh suit of the person robbed or from whom the goods were stolen in the manor or with the said goods in his possession, as upon him or about him, anciently termed backberende or hondhabende. And an outfangthief is one that neither is tenant or other living within such manor but apprehended therein upon such pursuit and in such manner as is aforesaid).

The second was a trial in or by appeal commenced at the suit of the party, either by bill or writ (which in case the party died or was non-suit the king might prosecute and was if the appellee were acquitted to give him damages). For the party ravished, maimed, robbed or whose goods were stolen, and the wife (or if there were no wife, the next man of kin) of any person murdered, might (& yet may) have their remedies against the offenders by appeal, if they sued in time, were not barred in such suit, or discontinued not the same. And the judgement of death thereupon given, because[45] that & restitution to the stolen goods were the only effects of the party's suit, the king's majesty was not to pardon, so as upon the party's prayer it was notwithstanding to be executed. But in case[46] they neglected their time, were barred in such suit or discontinued the same, or from the first prosecuted such felony but as trespass or compounded the matter, then in the cases of rape, robbery & larceny the king's counsel learned in the law or any of them or any other might (as the party grieved now for the most part do) prosecute the offenders by way of indictment (which run in the king's name & is therefore called the king's suit) as in the case of murder any of them might, by virtue of the statute, from the first.

Which was the third & last way of such trial, and is now become the only way used. {And the statute of 21 Henry VIII, c. 11 hath given like restitution of the stolen goods to the owner of the goods or person robbed, after conviction of the felon (upon indictment) by the evidence by him given or procured to be given[47] as in appeal.}[48] And to speak my thoughts freely concerning the others' disuse, for the first way it was too precipitate & sudden to hold long in settled times, for therein the accused person lay open to the practice, malice or false oath of his accuser, unless we can think such evil unknown in their days. But some then held that the offence was to be so manifest that it could not be denied (and if so felons had as much ingenuity in those days as they have impudence in ours). But some further held that the felon was at one time or other to have confessed the fact before honest men or such as could record it, and that if any felon had once so confessed his offence he could never after deny it but was taken to be in the same case as if he had been taken in the manor. But I conceive this first way was chiefly in use either during eyres, when there were justice seats or gaol deliveries in the same counties but once in seven years, because they would not suffer known & manifest offenders (when any in ordinary offices might judge) to lie in the gaol to corrupt others, of or against whom there was only suspicion, which required a careful & judicious trial & determination. Or else when the kingdom was filled with more thieves & villeins [sic] than free & honest men could well awe and keep under.

And from the second way men (though long violent in it) were at last discouraged because every appellee had (& yet may have) his choice to try the issue, either by jury or combat (& men grew loath to venture their lives against desperate felons who if vanquished were forthwith to be hanged). And next, for that if any such appellee chose to be tried by jury, the appellor (being a party) could be no witness and then the offences were hard to be proved. But lastly & I conceive chiefly, because the appellee upon his acquittal had damages in that suit or might recover them by action against the appellor. And if the appeal were judged malicious, the appellor was also to be imprisoned for a year & to be grievously fined to the king. And because it is the main & chief work not only of you but also of this court to discover & try offenders prosecuted at the king's suit, I shall here declare unto you the rise & course of such prosecutions.[49]

All this county, and I think I may as truly say all counties & places in this kingdom, were anciently divided into hundreds, and they subdivided into leets, so as there was scarce any town which was not within the jurisdiction of some court leet. And such towns as were not in any such leet were within the jurisdiction of the sheriff's turn. And the first of these was anciently to be held every three weeks and the last of them every solar month. But by Magna Carta it was provided that each of them should be held but twice in the year, within a month after Easter & within a month after Michaelmas in the place accustomed, & by 31 Edward III c. 5. And in all turns & leets every inhabitant (as well suitor as leeter) respectively were & are to be present & perform their services. And an homage or jury of twelve men or more (whereof each in turn had 20s. a year in freehold or 26s. 8d. in copyhold) were & are always in each turn & leet to be sworn to present or indict all offenders for every their offences within the cognizance of such turn or leet (wherein the death of man was & is excepted). But for such death upon every occasion the coroners of each county or place or one of them made & yet make inquiry by an inquest of twelve sworn men of the neighbourhood to the place of such death, upon the view of the body slain, how & by whom he came by such death. And lest there might be such offences unknown to such homage or jury, the chief constables & tithingmen & every of their whole tithings in every turn, and the petty constables in every leet, were & are to be particularly sworn to inform, inquire & present, as in some places they are sworn upon the homage or jury. And lest the knowledge of some offences might escape all these or their knowledges might be but imperfect, there were & to this day are, immediately after the charge given, three proclamations made for any that can inform of any felony, breach of the peace, or other thing given in charge to come forth to be heard. And if any do come forth they are forthwith sworn to give in evidence the truth, the whole truth, & nothing but the truth. And as before Magna Carta all felonies (death of man as I told you only excepted) and whatsoever were then held to be nuisances were heard & determined in turns & leets, so after that they only took presentments or indictments of or for the same, which after-statutes provided should be by roll indented and the jurors or indicters thereto to affix their seals. And one of them at the next sessions was to show one part of the indenture & there the undersheriff or steward was to deliver in the other. And heretofore at justices' seats in eyres, & since at general gaol deliveries, the coroners delivered the presentments & indictments of all kinds of manslaughters & all abjurations of felons & all outlawries, and at such eyres heretofore, & sessions & gaol deliveries since, the offenders were tried & one way or other thence delivered.

But whether it was that jurors in turns & leets did not diligently & truly make presentment of offences; or that the undersheriff & stewards did not draw them up sufficiently & in due form of law; or because offenders took notice of the presentments of themselves when so made and withdrew themselves or fled for their offences; or for that when presentments were duly made none would at the trials give evidence for the king against the offenders; or for that there then were diverse offences which neither leets nor yet turns have or ever had jurisdiction of and some were thought to require quicker dispatch than they could give; or whether it was for all or any of these reasons with or without other or for other, I certainly know not. But certain I am that after-statutes did give powers to justices of the peace out of sessions to hear & determine some few small & new made offences whose pains & penalties are of little value. Yet of any of them no offender is to be convicted but either by his own free confession of his offence before some justice of the peace, or by some such justice's hearing or view of the same, or by proof thereof made before some such justice by the testimony upon oath of one credible witness at the least. And another statute did also require every justice of the peace, upon complaint of any who were hurt or grieved in anything to be in any wise heard, determined or executed by such justice, forthwith to give remedy to such complainant. And other statutes did also[50] empower every justice of the peace, before whom any felonious offender should be brought, to take the examination of the offender & commit him, or if he were bailable with another such justice (one of them being of the quorum) to bail him; and to take the informations of them who should bring him or who could testify anything material to prove the offence; and to bind such informers & witnesses to give in evidence against the offender at his trial; and to certify such examination, informations, bond or recognizance where the offender should be tried.

By virtue whereof I conceive that as such as have been committed have been already tried where the common gaol for this county is kept & where this quarter sessions began, so here will be the offences of diverse accordingly certified, and the offenders will come in or be brought in here to have their trials. In order whereunto principally you for this grand inquest & other for the petty juries have been summoned. Principally, I said, for that you have also now to bring in your own presentment, and they are also now to try such as have come in upon sessions process & traversed their indictments. {And now for the legal presenting or indicting of such offences as have been committed in this division of our county and have not yet been so presented or indicted, and for the trials of such offenders as at the sessions of the peace held for this division heretofore have been or now shall be presented and indicted, you for this grand inquest and others for the petty juries have been formerly summoned and you have now been here called.}[51] And you upon your appearance have been sworn, and I thank you for your so ready & full an appearance, which shall be to me an hopeful argument that you will be as careful to perform your oaths, which either expressly or impliedly were that you should diligently inquire & true presentment make of all such matters and things as you should have in charge by this court.

Who by me do accordingly charge you so to inquire & present all high treasons, misprisions of high treason, petty treasons, murders, manslaughters, witchcrafts, buggeries, rapes, robberies, burglaries, burning any other's house or barn with corn, grand larcenies, petty larcenies & other felonies whatsoever. Praemunires, misprisions of felony, theftboots, negligent escapes, getters of money or other things by false letters or tokens, refusing or dissuading any to take any lawful oath when duly tendered or maintaining that the taking of an oath in any case whatsoever is altogether unlawful; profane cursing & swearing, perjuries, conspiracies, forgeries. All going or riding armed (especially any of the late disbanded armies), affrays or anything done in terror of the people, menaces, assaults (especially such assault or affray as any servant, workman, or labourer have willfully & maliciously made upon master, mistress, dame or any other person having the charge of such workers or work), batteries, blooddraughts (especially in any the king's courts or courts of record), mayhems. Striking or drawing any weapon to strike in any church or churchyard, the keeping any fair or market in the latter of them, the disturbing of purpose any licensed preacher in his open sermon in either of them, the rescuing any such disturber being apprehended, the parish where any such disturbance hath been made that hath suffered such disturber to escape unapprehended. Quakers to the number of five or more of sixteen years of age or upwards that have assembled together at any time since the 24th day of March 1662 in one place, being none of their habitation, under pretence of joining in a religious worship not authorized by the laws of this realm. Riots, routs, unlawful assemblies, forcible entries & detainers, common barratries, maintenances, champerties, embraceries, jurors taking to give their verdict. Exactions, extortions (especially in sheriffs, in coroners, in ordinaries about wills & administrations or in ministers for mortuaries or corpses present). All annoyances in & decays of bridges & highways, all nuisances & other annoyances, as casting dung or filth into any ditch, river or place to the infecting of the air or prejudicing the healths of the inhabitants, the not cleansing & keeping open of common gutters, drains or sewers, the stopping up of windows or lights, the obstructing, putting by or encroaching upon any ways, passages or paths, especially such as lead to church, mill or market.

Forestallers, engrossers, regrators; unlawful balances, weights & measures; goldsmiths, pewterers, brasiers, badgers or kidders, bakers, brewers, coopers, drovers, butchers, fishmongers, millers, maltsters, tanners, curriers, shoemakers, tilemakers, clothiers, carders, spinsters, weavers, fullers and dyers failing in their respective duties in or about their several occupations. Conspiracies of tradesmen, artificers or labourers to sell victual or to work at certain rates or prices, or to work but at certain hours or times, or to do but so much in a day, or not to end work other have begun & left, or taking work & leaving the same unfinished; refusing to take some and undue taking of others for apprentices; servants, masters, mistresses & dames as to undue retaining into, departing or putting out of service, or giving or taking of excessive wages. {And that the offences in undue retaining of servants and in giving & taking of excessive wages may be the better prevented, that 'tis commanded & expected that chief constables should duly & yearly keep their petty sessions. And because 'tis feared many of them may not well understand their duties in this particular, 'tis also desired that two justices of the peace in and for each hundred would without fail be at the petty sessions that are to be held before next Michaelmas after or towards at [sic] the end of harvest, to enter, direct or countenance them & to curb & restrain the insolence of such as shall obstruct or oppose.}[52]

Taverners, innkeepers, alehousekeepers & victualers not observing the law or their articles, and all recognizances entered by them or any of them or by any other and forfeited. Tipplers, drunkards, keepers of gaming houses & gamesters playing therein, and all others playing at unlawful games, sports & exercises used on the Lord's day, and all other profanations thereof by waggoners, carmen, carriers, drovers, butchers & shoemakers. The depraving & despising of the sacrament of the body & blood of Christ; sayers or singers & willing hearers of mass; procurers, contrivers & publishers of libels or fond fantastical and false prophecies.

Cottages at any time or times since & contrary to the statute of 31 Elizabeth c. 7 erected or converted & for every month or more continued, and inmates or more families than one contrary to the law placed or willingly suffered for every month or more in any cottage. Unlicensed alehouses & such as lodge strangers in upland towns they will not answer for; rogues & vagabonds and all those that by the law are to be punished as such; the not keeping of Winchester watch and the not following of hues & cries. Common informers upon any penal law making composition before or by pretence of process, without the consent of some of his majesty's courts at Westminster, or after process before answer, or without the consent of the court, where the suit is depending after answer; and the clerk who maketh out any such process before the information be exhibited in the proper office or to the due person. And the day, month & year of the exhibiting thereof be noted thereon (for till then it is not of record) and shall not on such process have endorsed the informer's name & the statute upon which the information is grounded. All contempts in transgressing any statute whereof this court hath cognizance, or in not due performing or executing process, warrants & lawful commands of any court of general quarter sessions, or of any justices of the peace at any private sessions or meeting & assembly, or of any such justice or justices by virtue of their office though elsewhere. Undersheriffs, bailiffs, stewards (as well of leets as turns), constables, gaolers, governors of bridewells & other officers who have presumed to misbehave themselves in their offices or have been in the same lukewarm, slack or negligent. All destruction of gentlemen's game and all unlawful use thereof; the having or keeping of unlawful guns and the unlawful using or shooting in any such or in any other [sic]. And all other contempts, forces, frauds, deceits and oppressions, and all and every other trespass & trespasses and offence & offences whatsoever, and all & every the offender & offenders whosoever in & about them & every or any of them, throughout this my charge mentioned, who and which are here by law & of right inquirable and presentable.

And amongst them, you are more particularly now to inquire & present whosoever ought to have been taxed and, without just cause, willingly by any words, coven or craft have escaped the taxation or taxations of each or either two of the four entire subsidies lately granted by the temporalty to his majesty that now is; and whosoever that was taxed to each or either of them & have got of such taxation or taxations abated by deposing upon oath that his or her estate (in lands & goods or either of them) was of less value at the time of such oath than in truth the same was then of. For such as shall be found so to have concealed their estates are, besides what they have already paid with or after such abatement, to pay as much as they were taxed at before their abatement so gained. And such as so escaped taxing are to pay double to what they ought to have been taxed at.

Which that you gentlemen may now the better do, you are speedily & seriously to consider your duty in this service to which you have been called and even now by solemn oath thus charged. Which consists either in matter of fact or in matter of law, and I conceive charges were at first principally made for the directions of jurors in matters of law, and you shall have that more fully from the officer in court in the bills to be brought unto you ready drawn, and you may have the same help in whatsoever you would otherwise present & indict. And for matter of fact, you ordinarily perform that either upon the testimony of witness upon oath or upon the knowledge of you or some or any of you (the knowledge of any of you declared to the residue being by them to be admitted as the testimony of such witness) or else upon both. And in which you (who are therein neither to regard rich or poor, friend or foe (as such) but the truth & merit of the case) are to proceed with great exactness & strictness, being the eyes of this court for the impartial discovery of all such offences & of the offenders in the same, that they may be according to the law charged with & upon lawful convictions be duly punished for the same. Which unless you first perform on your parts, we cannot do ours, but upon your performance I hope I may clearly declare that we on our parts will not be wanting.

And herein I shall give you the directions & caution mentioned in your oath, that you present nothing for hatred, malice or evil will, fear, favour, reward or hope of reward, for herein you (and the same throughout are as true of ourselves in our concerns) are not to remember any private grudges or return or requite former injuries, much less take vengeance with despiteful heart for old hatred. You are not to afflict the just or take a bribe, for a gift doth blind the eyes of the wise & pervert the matters of the righteous. Neither are you to favour any vice for the person's sake or to hate any person for his vice, nor in judgement to respect persons, but to hear the small as well as the great and not be afraid of the face of man, for the judgement is God's.

And because I lately found, at those sessions where I last gave the charge and where a woman was indicted for the assault & battery of a constable and the offence proved to the satisfaction of the grand inquest, that they would not have found the bill. For being questioned about it by the court, one of them made answer, She pulled him but a little by the hair, and it was but for a little chimney money, and could not but acknowledge that she thereby rescued the distress. Therefore I hold it necessary to subjoin that you ought to take as great care to perform your duty in lesser offences as in great, for your office & your oaths oblige you equally in & to either. And from impunity for small offences, offenders are encouraged unto greater. And that you ought not to account any offence small which is committed against the king's majesty in his person, authority, revenue or aids, or any of his officers in the execution of his or their office. For the first two are either high treason or verging nearly thereon. And once from the two last (as the mentioned case clearly was) did arise in this kingdom one of the most general & violent rebellions that ever did interrupt or disturb the peace thereof, wherein this county & Suffolk (then & long after under one sheriff) had then more than their full share. For out of these parts were then gathered together by one Wrawe 50,000 men who were at last overthrown at North Walsham, being led by one Littiser, who called himself the king of the commons and was afterward hanged, as he well deserved.

And for the office of a constable, it is very ancient, & though of late the same hath been unreasonably depressed by putting it upon the most inconsiderable and unfit persons that could be picked, yet is still an office of the king's and the chief office of every town that is not incorporated and hath diverse authorities very necessary to be put in practice for the quiet & profit of the kingdom. And I hope it will not be long ere provision shall be made to have that office executed by persons well qualified and fit to manage it. And truly gentlemen, taking it as granted that the bills to be brought unto you shall contain the matter of law (and I shall expect that my so easy admission thereof will henceforth increase the care of him is employed therein), neither you or the petty juries are to find or not find the same or the offenders guilty or not guilty at your or their wills or discretions, much less for others' importunities or satisfactions, but only according to your or their knowledges or the confessions or proofs of the facts or at least of the strong & violent presumptions thereof.

And if I thought not the duty of your offices & the conscience of your oaths sufficient obligations to persuade or enforce you, I would yet add these motives. There hath been great liberty granted or taken during our late civil wars and too much connivance at offenders, many men's consciences being loath then to act anything against them more than necessity enforced while they knew or feared they had no good authority by or under which they could justify it. And this hath much increased

& emboldened offenders. And the armies lately disbanded have afforded many too old & lazy to learn and labour, and too likely and ready to beg and steal. Yea & a new race of loose or runaway rogues are lately sprung up, who were scarce ever or never well-fixed in any lawful course of life. And both these at your doors pretend themselves to be shipwrecked men, and if that be questioned, they will straight intimate it by testimonials (commonly called passes) which you may know to be (by themselves or others) forged or counterfeited, by the long time allowed them therein for their passage, which is not usually above two miles a day, whereas they ought to go ten miles a day by the direct road & not by such indirect traverses as they make about the country; by the bad English & unclerklike hands they be wrote in, and by the hands or at least the seals of the justices or chief magistrates set or pretended to be set unto them.

For persons of those qualities never seal but with their coats of arms or crests well cut in silver, gold, steel or stone, and always set the impressions fairly, whereas the seals in their forged or counterfeited passes are (if they were ever made with such coats or crests) taken off of other papers & then fixed to their passes, which may be easily discerned either by the wax or paper or both, whether the wax be hard or soft, for if the wax of an old seal be heated after the impression made thereon, it is easy to be seen. And besides it cannot be heated so much as will make it hang firmly to the pass, but it will quite put out & deface, or, according to the degree of the heat, dull or abate the impression of or upon the seal. And if they keep the impression fair, they must have put on the seal so cold that it will not hang upon the pass but so as upon the least stirring it about the seal, the seal will come off. And the paper of the pass (on its backside) will not then be so pressed down as when a seal is truly sealed thereon. And if they put the seals on with other wax, the seals will stand high and the differences in the colours, hardness or softness of the waxes may be easily observed. Or else they be passes were sometimes good, being only altered in their dates, which may be easily seen in the pass and concluded against all excuses, if the alterations be made with another hand and ink. But most of their counterfeited & forged passes be commonly sealed with halfpenny seals meanly cut in brass or horn, with tops of inkhorns or pitiful cuts in sticks or wood.[53] (And by the way, take notice that every soldier or mariner or other person pretending to be either, wandering with any forged or counterfeited testimonial, known to him to be so, is a felon & is not to have benefit of clergy.)

But if you cannot discover them by any of these to be rogues, if you will but look carefully upon the brawn of their left thumbs, you shall seldom miss of brands there made with an hot iron in form of a great Roman 'T', the certain signs or marks of their former thieveries. Carefully, I said, for you may find that in some their brands have been but slightly set, or when well set, bit or cut out, but then there is a scar. And they all use their utmost care & art to conceal them, by dirtying their hands or laying pitch upon the brands, which they will pretend to be done by mending their shoes or handling the ship ropes or otherwise. And thus these rogues hawk about the country. First they get your money & then they filch your goods. Or if they have fit numbers & opportunity, while some beg at your doors, others of them are putting up what they see abroad. And thus they find a more easy & profitable way to live by than by working, and this (unless some effectual courses shall be taken for prevention) they scarce will ever leave or give over until the gallows either mend or end them.

And from hence I might now show a great necessity that everyone in his place should duly help towards the execution of the laws against offenders, and more particularly now press the execution of those laws which in one of the last ages were made for such a time as this and whose use & practice then were found successful. In which I conceive privy searches to be the chief, made generally throughout the whole county or division in the same night, which by the statute ought to have been & yet continue to be twice in every year & oftener in case of need. And sure there was scarce ever more need than now. Thereby the country will inform themselves who are rogues and soon learn their own power to punish them (as they may and ought without our trouble), which if duly executed will soon reform them or rid the country of them and save themselves not only their misbestowed alms for the right objects of their charity, the poor of their parish, but also their forfeitures, which they incur by so relieving such rogues, which if a constable is 40s., if any other person is 10s. due to such poor upon conviction for every such offence.

And now as I have discovered some means to prevent secret pickeryes[54] & private thefts, so I had intended to have showed some means for preventing of open force & public violence. Which should have been by looking to the due taking of apprentices, that they who were intended by the law for husbandry and country employments might be brought up therein and not in other manufactures & trades (contrary to the law), wherein already so many have been & yet are that they neither could or can live one by another (on their trades) but have been forced to take up fighting for an employment, when the meanwhile the plow even stood and yet stands still for want of hands to manage it. But time hath prevented me. Therefore I shall by the way only give you notice that each master who unduly taketh any apprentice forfeiteth ten pounds, and he that is so taken setting up & using the trade or employing in the trade any so taken forfeiteth forty shillings for every month.

And so close all with this brief exhortation. That as you have sworn in the presence & name of the same God (who will not hold them guiltless who take his name in vain [and] is discerner of the thoughts & intents of the heart, and that not only when they are but long before they be) diligently & truly to inquire & present all such matters & things as you now have in charge, so that in his name & fear, as well for the full & due observance of your oaths as for the satisfaction & preservation of the king's laws & peace, the defence & safeguard of the subject's persons & estates and the discouragement & punishment of offenders & offences (considerations to be ever highly esteemed by all just & honest men) you would now do the same faithfully and with a perfect heart. D[ei?] G[ratia?] R[obert] D[oughty].[55]

Notes to Appendix I

1. Aylsham 304. RD apparently delivered this charge, internally dateable to these dates, on 7 August 1662 at Fakenham.
2. The passages in braces, appended at the end of the charge, apparently belong here.
3. 'N' in the margin.
4. 'Droves of' is deleted.
5. A boot extending to the middle of the leg.
6. A kind of slipper.
7. 'Using' is deleted.
8. 'Two lawful accusers' is deleted.
9. Advance soldiers clearing a way for the main force of an army.
10. 'It' is deleted.
11. Adherents or abettors.
12. 'Edward' is deleted.
13. 'After or' is deleted here.
14. 'Offences' is deleted here.
15. 'Said' is deleted.
16. An 's' is deleted as well as the words 'or servant'.
17. A dike meant to keep fen waters out of Marshland in western Norfolk.
18. The border of a country.
19. Illegible word deleted.
20. Partly legible deletion of several words. The sentence appears to have read 'But in all other and lesser felonies, all present but the principal offender are but accessories.'
21. Autrefois acquit or convict were defendant's pleas alleging previous trial and either acquittal or conviction for the same offence.
22. Illegible word deleted.
23. Barratry is persisting in or inciting to litigation.
24. Abetting litigation by a party with no interest in the proceedings or who acts from improper motive.
25. Assisting in the prosecution of a suit in which one is not naturally concerned on condition of receiving a share of the property in dispute.
26. Efforts to influence a jury corruptly.
27. Aylsham 304. This charge is nearly identical with one entitled 'A Charge provided to have been spoken unto the good men at Walsingham, 22 January Anno Domini 1662 [sic] per me RD,' ibid. It is likely that RD here employed New Style dating and was referrring to a charge scheduled for delivery at Twelfth-night sessions in 1662, a date when his notebook indicates he was ill. Several passages included in the charge transcribed here were appended to the one of January, as if to be added during revision.
28. 'As casting dung or filth into any ditch, river or place to the infecting of the air or prejudicing the healths of the inhabitants, the not cleansing & keeping open of common gutters, drains or sewers, the stopping up of windows or lights, the putting by or encroaching

upon any ways, passages or paths (especially such as lead to church, mill or market)' is scored through in the text.

29. One word deleted.
30. One word deleted.
31. Several words deleted.
32. Aylsham 304.
33. 'Before' is deleted.
34. 'His' is deleted.
35. One word deleted.
36. One word deleted.
37. Persons taken from those present in court to serve on a jury when the original panel became deficient in number.
38. A writ of arrest.
39. A writ commanding a sheriff to summon a defendant to appear and deliver himself up on pain of outlawry.
40. One word deleted.
41. An accident or casualty of a mixed character and not purely accidental.
42. 'That no' is deleted.
43. A pack or wallet; a travelling bag.
44. 'And' is deleted.
45. Several words deleted.
46. This phrase is written twice, with 'in case' deleted.
47. 'By him' is deleted.
48. The passage in braces, which is flagged by an 'X' in the text, is contained on a slip of paper tipped into the gathering at this point.
49. Doughty indicates in his notebook, 4 August 1664, that when he read this charge at quarter sessions, he began at this point in the text.
50. 'After' is deleted.
51. The passage in braces appears on a slip of paper tipped into the gathering at this point. The text on the paper continues as follows, repeating the sense of the main text: 'And upon your call you have appeared (and I thank you for your so ready and full an appearance), & upon your appearance your foreman hath been expressly and the residue of you have been implicitly sworn to make diligent inquiry and true presentment of all such matters and things as you should have in charge by this court.'
52. The passage in braces, which appears on a slip of paper tipped into the gathering at an earlier point, apparently belongs here.
53. 'Or with an old wife's butter print' is deleted.
54. Petty thefts.
55. There follow the texts of passages from John 7:51, Luke 16:2, Matthew 22:12-13, Genesis 3:9-19, I Corinthians 15:22, I John 2:1-2, I Corinthians 15:56-57, Galatians 3:24, and Ezekiel 16:49-50.

APPENDIX II:

Robert Doughty's Charge to the Tax Commissioners of South Erpingham, North Erpingham, North Greenhoe and Holt Hundreds

February 1664[1]

Gentlemen and neighbours,

That the ends of all governments are the good of the governed and the security and support of the governors was a truth, if not agreed on, assented to on all sides during our late uncivil civil wars when almost all things were controverted. And then the difference about these ends was only put in their order, which should have precedency or was first in intention, until some men's self-preservation, or worse ends disguised under that pretense, made them warp from the same. For which most of them have had passed upon them the judgement of the law, and diverse of them have been since executed according to such judgements. And our kings (as well ancient as modern) have in their straits and necessities, which their own revenues (though great) could not sufficiently provide against, had constant recourses (first or last) to their people in parliament. Who from time to time by several ways and means have respectively[2] afforded them aids and reliefs, sometimes by enabling their kings out of the king's own, sometimes by shortening the king's expences and charges, and sometimes by acts for resuming the lands and liberties [which] had been aliened and conveyed from the crown, but for the most part by granting unto their kings out of the people's estates[3] either perpetual or temporary supplies.

The perpetual were customs, first of wools, woolfells and leather transported, then of wools manufactured or draped here and transported hence. And the temporary were tonnage and poundage, sometimes at several rates, sometimes for years, but in our last ages granted our kings for their lives. And when these would not satisfy the occasions, fifteenths and tenths (commonly called tasks), which, though when they were first granted they were set upon men in the towns they dwelt in according to the then value of their goods and so [were] uncertain, yet soon after they were made certain and settled upon the towns according to the values of the goods of the dwellers therein, and thence until their last [were] levied by a land rate. Wherein I have found that they rated (at the least) at three unequal proportions, the lord of the manor being about ten groats, five shillings or a noble, which bore no near proportion with the tenants, who paid near two pence by the acre for their freeholds and had about a fourth part thereof abated in their copyhold. And as well for these inequalities as for that diverse ancient and great towns had since decayed, others out of their ruins or otherwise had been raised or increased, some the seas had wasted and others it had washed away, and chiefly for that many cities, towns, places and persons stood privileged by grant, office or prescription from paying to the same, that charge did at last lie upon so few, and that so unevenly, that it made men (if not unable) at least unwilling longer to continue the same.

And then parliaments began to aid their kings, partly with tasks and partly with subsidies, and from the seventh year of the reign of the late King James over England (wherein the last task was granted) with subsidies only. Which then were and yet are either of the spiritualty, which now are and long time have been of four shillings in every pound of the nine parts of church livings and ecclesiastical promotions as they stand valued in the king's books, made about the six and twentieth year of the reign of King Henry the eighth, but were sometimes of six shillings and eight shillings in the pound. Or else of the temporalty, which so far as I have seen always was and yet is of eight groats in every pound on goods and of four shillings in every pound on lands, with some additions or increase from aliens' and recusants' lands, goods and polls. And though in the two first subsidies that I have, the utmost true values of lands and goods were designed, which the assessors were then to certify upon their oaths, yet in all after times they did from time to time certify the values with considerable abatements. And such abatements in continuance of time became so many and in the end so great that the Long Parliament, finding it took six subsidies to raise what they had expected from four, and that each two of the last four fell in value exceedingly below the two next before going, waived and declined all[4] further use of subsidies and imposed a certain sum of about £400,000, in which this county (with Norwich included) was under £24,450 and yet (as I have computed it) was surcharged therein above £9690. And thenceforth during the whole time of the wars, and until the last eighteen monthly assessments were levied, most impositions and levies made have been of sums certain by the week, month or otherwise, wherein this county hath long borne proportions far above its true value, notwithstanding the continued cares and endeavours of the successive parliament members of this county to remedy and prevent the same.

And now as the king's majesty is by God's blessing quietly settled in his throne and government and hath paid off and disbanded the armies and hath declared his desires that all things should return and run in their ancient course and channels, and as the parliament now prorogued in the act for the eighteen monthly assessments hath also declared that no more moneys should be raised by such assessments, so before their prorogation they provided for the known, weighty and important occasions which did press his majesty by unanimously presenting him with four entire subsidies of the temporalty.

And the due taxing and levying the last two of them is now our present work, who amongst others are named commissioners for this county in the act of parliament made for that end and since amongst others by virtue thereof assigned unto this limit. Which being to be taxed before the first day of the next March, and certified into the king's exchequer before the fourteenth day of the next April, and paid into the king's receipt there to his use before the first day of the next May, that there might be no obstruction or delay caused or given thereunto on our parts, we have according to the said act duly issued our several precepts unto you personally to be and appear before us at this day and place.

And we thank you for your so full and general appearances, and we will hope that ye will continue the like care and diligence until ye shall have performed you [sic] charges. Which are, and we do charge every of you (except Mr Baxter whom (for his sickness) we have discharged), in and for your own respective hundreds only, that by all convenient ways and means (except corporal oath) you inquire after the usual manner of the utmost and best value of the substance of every person spiritual and temporal now dwelling and abiding in any of the towns or other places within your respective hundreds or having his or her chief resort unto any of the said towns or other places, or being out of this kingdom or Wales, now have any goods, chattels, lands, tenements, fees, annuities or other profits there, or being now out of this kingdom and Wales or far from the place where he shall be known (who is there best known or) had there his last abiding within England; and of the utmost and best value of the substance there of every fraternity, guild, corporation, mystery, brotherhood and commonalty corporate or not corporate within the king's dominions; either in (what is generally termed) goods, though here it only contains coin, plate, stock of merchandise, all manner of corn and grain, household stuff and other goods movable as well within this realm as without, and all sums of money to him or them owing whereof he or they trust in his or their conscience to be surely paid, worth three pounds or more in subsidy account. But you are thereout to deduct such sums of money as he or they do owe and in his or their conscience intend truly to pay, and the apparel of the bodies of every such person, their wives and children (saving jewels, gold, silver, stone and pearl). Or else in (what is generally termed) lands, which here contains any honours, castles, manors, lands, tenements, rents, services, hereditaments, annuities, fees, corrodies or other yearly profits in fee simple, fee tail, for term of life, term of years, by execution or copy of court roll, as well within ancient demesne and other places privileged as elsewhere, of the yearly value of twenty shillings or upwards in subsidy account. But thereout you are to deduct likewise all lands and tenements chargeable to the dismes of the clergy and yearly wages due to servants for their service (except the wages of the king's servants taking five pounds yearly wages or more), whether such lands or goods be in him or them or in any other to his or their use and wheresoever the same lands or goods be or lie.

But here lest you should mistake, before I proceed further in your charges I shall let you know that you are not now to assess any person or community for his or their lands who at or to the former two of these four entire subsidies were assessed for his or their goods, and that you are not to inquire after those lands that are to be charged by another act but not by this,[5] as the lands and tenements before mentioned to be chargeable to the dismes of the clergy, they being charged to four subsidies granted to his majesty by the spiritualty. Nor those persons who are to be charged by this act but not by us, as all persons of the estate of a baron or baroness (of this kingdom) or other estate above, they being to be taxed by persons of great honours particularly named in this act, or any seven or more of them, for their freehold or value according to the common rates of this act, and their taxations to be levied by collectors appointed by the lord chancellor or lord keeper for the time being. Nor those persons' lands and goods which are neither to be charged by this act or the other, which I shall endeavour succinctly thus to enumerate unto ye.

Neither the inhabitants nor resiants of Scotland, Ireland, Jersey and Guernsey or any of them for the lands or goods they or any other to their use have within them or any of them; or for any fees or wages any of the said inhabitants have of the king's majesty for their attendance and doing service to him within them or any of them; nor the English inhabitants or resiants at the passing of this act within the liberties of Romney Marsh during their resiance there, nor the inhabitants or resiants for the most part of the year before the taxing and assessing of these four entire subsidies, within the five ports corporate or any their members incorporated or united to the said five ports or any of them, during such their resiance in the said five ports or any their members aforesaid; nor orphans or infants within the age of one & twenty years born within any the king's majesty's dominions for goods or chattels to them left or bequeathed, nor the goods chattels, jewels and ornaments of churches and chapels which have been ordained and used in churches & chapels for the honour and service of Almighty God, nor any goods or chattels of the poor knights of the College of Windsor, nor the revenues appointed for their sustentation, nor the goods or lands of any hospital, maison de dieu, or spital house used for relief of poor people; (nor such apparel of the body of any person, his wife and children, as I have already told you were to be deducted out of his goods); nor the lands and goods of either of the colleges of Winchester and Eton or of any college, hall or hostel within either of the universities of Oxford and Cambridge; nor the goods or lands of any free grammar school within England and Wales, or the goods of any reader, schoolmaster or scholar or any graduate resiant or remaining for study without fraud or coven, within any the said universities & colleges of Oxford and Cambridge; nor[6] any of them nor[7] any of their servants tending daily upon any of them are to be charged to these four entire subsidies by this act.

And now to proceed, that you therewithal likewise inquire who of such persons as be of such substance be popish recusants convicted or indicted for popish recusancy and not discharged, or aliens and strangers born out of the king's dominions (as well denizens as others), and who of such persons as be not of such substance now be, or before the taxation of these two last subsidies shall be, popish recusants convicted of seventeen years of age, or being of one & twenty years of age have not received the holy communion within one year last past, or be such aliens & strangers and of seven years of age or above, and who is the master or person with whom any such alien and stranger now abideth. And that you thereupon as near as may be or shall come to your knowledge (without respect to former taxations) truly and respectively present and certify in writing after the usual manner before the commissioners at the house of Richard Greenewood, being the sign of the Black Boy in Aylsham, on this day fortnight, by eight of the clock in the morning, the names and surnames of all and every such person and persons having such substance in lands or goods, and who of them be such popish recusants convicted or indicted and not discharged as first aforesaid, or be such aliens and strangers as first aforesaid, and the names of every such community having there such substance as aforesaid, and the utmost and best value of such substance either in lands or goods of every such person and community, and the names and surnames of all and every such person & persons having no such substance in lands or goods, who be or shall be as foresaid popish recusants convicted of seventeen years of age, or being of one & twenty years of age have not received the holy communion within one year last past, or be such aliens and strangers of seven years of age or above, and the name and surname of every master or other person with whom any such alien & stranger now abideth. And that you respectively do all these things in your several[8] hundreds, without any concealment, love, favour, affection, dread or malice, that the commissioners may thereupon proceed to the taxing of such persons and communities by their lands, goods or polls, by virtue of this act and according to the direction and true meaning of the same.

And that you might be the fitter to perform this charge, we did take care ye should be such persons and so equally disposed in and throughout your hundreds that one or other of you might of yourselves have some knowledge of every of the parts of your own whole hundreds, which you may confirm and increase by the help of such sub-informations as you will receive of your several towns of the names, surnames and qualifications of such persons and communities as you are to inquire of therein, and of the utmost best values of their substance in lands or goods, if you will apply your special care to discover and observe in what proportion or proportions each town shall undervalue her inhabitants. And first reduce them all to exact values and then give every of them an abatement according to the course in subsidies, which if you do not, but shall admit as true whatsoever each town shall inform you, these gross inconveniences will thereon ensue. Towns without doubt will make one abatement at least and you another, and both or all will render the taxed sums so inconsiderable to answer those weighty and important occasions for which (as I have told you) they were given, that subsidiary aids will again lose their esteem and be set by, and then new ways will be devised which may hazard more prejudice, or the old will be revived, which will renew our certain loss. Which the commissioners of this county have so clearly foreseen and been so desirous to prevent that they generally raised themselves at the last taxation far above the precedents in the times of King James and King Charles the first, by which these four entire subsidies, by the last proviso of this act, were to be regulated. And the commissioners for this limit then taxed themselves as much again as any commissioners here for like estates had been at any time for fifty years before. And yet of my knowledge diverse of them (after they heard commissioners in other limits had taxed themselves higher) did of themselves freely raise themselves some five pounds apiece, and others after other proportions as well higher as lower. And yet the hundred of South Erpingham then fell so low (when all the other hundreds in this limit were (more or less) over) that their taxation fell more than one hundred pounds short of what they in proportion had been in a taxation made in the first year of King Charles the first, as I after found in Mr Neave's estreat thereof. Now that there may well be in hundreds, and in some cases must be, some alterations, we do know. But that it should be by abatement and that so great as two-fifths, could not be without much connivance, to say no worse. Therefore now let it be repaired or if not repaired at least amended. And do you of the other hundreds take heed, that your books be not let down in the general or their total sums, and let those particulars you shall abate for just cause seen be again made up by those who you shall find were before either omitted or else undervalued, remembering all along that in a matter of great import you are now to do the king's work and not to serve yourselves and your friends.

And so we pass to the concerns chiefly of others, where this taxation shall be undermade, although there be as well provisions to raise those undervalued as to punish such as escape the taxation, with double value of what such ought to have been taxed at and further punishment at discretion. Yet I fear the same will scarce be timely seen and then the king will lose his dues, which I intend as a motive to you to let no person escape you and to certify values high enough. For on the other side, where the same shall be overmade, everyone justly and duly complaining thereof to two commissioners before the return of our certificate into the Exchequer may be heard and eased. And in regard we have more time allowed for this return than we had for the former, I think we shall appoint several days and places for several hundreds, when and where complainants may be examined upon their oaths, and their neighbours at discretion. And if you shall be then there, the truth may the more clearly be discovered and the abuse and loss of his majesty therein be the better prevented thereby. But if any by a false oath shall get abated, if within a year after such oath made it be proved by witnesses, confession or otherwise, that he or she was of better value than was declared upon the oath, the offender shall forfeit as much as he or she was taxed to pay.

For the payment of this taxation, an high collector is to be named, who is to have an estreat thereof and to enter bond or recognizance in double his charge for paying the same to his majesty's use, according to the said act, under pain of forfeiture of twenty pounds. And with his assent, under-collectors, who for each hundred are to have an estreat and are immediately upon delivery of the same, without any warrant but the delivery thereof and this act, to demand, gather and levy of every one the sum on him or her taxed, and for non-payment thereof to distrain each such person by his or her goods and chattels. And such distress to keep eight days at the owner's charge and then for non-payment thereof to sell the same after its appraisal by four, three, or two of the inhabitants where the distress be taken, and restore the overplus if any be. And to pay over their whole collections to the high collector at such times and places within this limit as he shall appoint, either of them the said high collector & under-collectors for themselves respectively detaining two pence in the pound for what he or they shall so collect, receive and pay over.

And now I think there is nothing more in this act necessary to be declared to you or them, unless it be that this act hath given us power upon any disobedience, willful omission, misdoing, contempt or neglect to impose for every offence forty shillings at least, which I hope there will be no cause to put in act, and that the high collector is to pay the commissioner or commissioners who have the ordering of the writings for him or them and clerks two pence in the pound. And that he hath power to distrain under-collectors who duly pay not over to him the money they shall have received with the only deduction of two pence in every[9] pound received and paid over. And that if any alien to defraud the king hath conveyed his lands or goods to his child or children born in this kingdom, that such child or children is or are to be charged for the same double to what aliens are by this act appointed to pay. Therefore certify also all such. And that aliens and recusants chargeable for their lands or goods by this act are to be taxed to these two subsidies ten shillings and eight pence in the pound for their goods and sixteen shillings in the pound for their lands, and all other chargeable recusants and aliens for their polls sixteen pence apiece, and all others whosoever five shillings and eight pence in the pound for their goods and eight shillings in the pound for their lands as they now are to be rated in the subsidy books.

But notwithstand [sic] for your better notice and more clear knowledge of what is required in and about this service, the act itself, to which I do and shall for more certainty rely, and to which I wish and advise you as occasion to have recourse, shall be forthwith read unto you, and then I shall direct you in the manner of your certificates, according to the true intent and meaning of the same.

But first, lest any should say now (as sometimes of old) here are four subsidies granted, but what beneficial laws are there made for the advantage of the realm or common profit of the people? I do take it to be my duty here to tell you all, that as our ancient kings by inviting hither and by encouraging with privileges here those foreigners who first taught our countrymen, who before that let their wools go over seas unwrought, those manufactures thereof which have since so usefully and profitably employed so many hands, that thence the meanest have ever since had certain livelihoods, and others have gained plentiful estates, so the king's majesty hath by an act passed at the last session of the parliament now prorogued, in like manner invited and encouraged any foreigners who will come hither to teach our countrymen to make linen, damasks, diapers and tapestries, choosing rather to be prejudiced in his customs (in which these commodities now bear high rates) than to omit or lose the means to employ more hands and to raise more credit and profit to this kingdom. And I could heartily wish those late disbanded soldiers bound to these new arts, who have either never gotten or else quite forgotten their former trades, and I fear otherwise will be too old to learn, too lazy to work, too proud to beg, and too ready to steal. And that those manufactures may be henceforth (as those of wools were of old) brought here to such perfection that the product of their rates inward at the present may be far exceeded by the product of their rates outward for the future. But this is not that I chiefly intended, for his majesty hath far exceeded this (copied from his ancestors) in another act passed at the same session, entitled An Act for the Encouragement of Trade, wherein is very much of a politician and of a good commonwealth's man, promising honour, plenty and prosperity unto this kingdom.

In the first place it gives great encouragements unto our tillage; next it provides that our husbandman shall not be undersold in corn or cattle brought from any other place or kingdom, and yet that this kingdom shall be provided for with corn in case of the high price thereof. Then it makes this kingdom the staple of all commodities growing in any English plantation and of all commodities whence soever to be shipped to any of them. Also it provides that nothing shall be shipped to or from them but in English-built shipping, whereof the master and three-quarters of the mariners are to be English (but Tangier and some few commodities are therein excepted). And lastly it provides that no fresh herrings, fresh cod or haddock, colefish or gulfish from the first day of August next shall be imported into England, Wales or Berwick but in English-built ships or belonging to England, Wales or Berwick, whereof the master and three-quarters of the mariners are to be English, and fished and navigated in the same, upon the pains of forfeiture of such commodities, fish, ships and vessels.

And truly the design of this act last mentioned is so high and noble that I can easily believe it to be one (at least) of those four particulars, discovered in his majesty's royal declaration of December 62, wherein he intended to give his good subjects the important marks of his care. And therefore I do earnestly desire and shall seriously expect that all persons as they be concerned or related in or to this service, or about these two subsidies, would now cheerfully return unto his majesty a suitable testimony of their dutiful affections[10] in the same, and by sessing them truly, taxing them justly and paying them duly, render unto Caesar the things that are Caesar's.

Directions for the manner of certificates and for under-collectors

First let the assessors of South Erpingham raise their book to its true value and no other let theirs down. Sess £20 per annum in lands [at] 20s. and £300 in goods [at] £3; [assess] an £100 per annum [at] £4 or £3 as the person's quality is, and after £3 in every £100 upwards, or otherwise higher or lower as will best make up the books.

Certify each half hundred apart by itself and keep the towns in each exactly on the alphabet. Divide the leaves of your books in four parts. In the first write the towns' names as aforesaid. In the two next, the names, surnames & qualifications of the persons & communities and their respective sessed sums. And next them write in the fourth the taxed sums, which are to be after the rates of 5s. 4d. in every pound for goods, and of 8s. in every pound for lands, but of such recusants and aliens (as be chargeable for lands or goods) double proportions, and of the residue of such recusants and aliens (as we by you inquire of) sixteen pence apiece for their polls.

Only write down the commissioners' & sessors' names & surnames in the towns where they dwell, with addition of commissioner or sessor, and leave their substances to be assessed and them to be taxed by the commissioners.

Certify lands first and therein first set persons, then communities' & town lands and then, and so for goods. After put recusants and then aliens for their polls, and the person with whom any such alien now abideth, and mixed not one with another.

Sum up your books and set your hands unto them.

For under-collectors

In their own hundreds they may without doubt distrain the goods of any person to be distrained, but I think not elsewhere without a particular warrant made under hand & seal of some commissioners. And such warrant they must also have (as the case shall require) to distrain the goods or in the lands of the farmer, debtor, factor, agent, heir or executor of or for any person etc.

Notes to Appendix II

1. Aylsham 304. The charge was probably delivered on 29 February 1664: see 'The taxation of...the last two of the four entire subsidies...rated and taxed at Aylsham...29 February 1664,' Aylsham 306. The subsidies assessed at this meeting were authorized by the statute of 15 Charles II, c. 10.
2. Several words deleted.
3. The phrase originally read 'their own particular estates'.
4. 'Any' is deleted.
5. 'Act' is deleted.
6. 'Or to' is deleted.
7. 'Or to' is deleted.
8. 'Respective' is deleted.
9. 'The' is deleted.
10. 'Therein and' is deleted.